MANAGING THE SURVIVAL
OF SMALLER COMPANIES

BY THE SAME AUTHORS

ENJOYING A PROFITABLE BUSINESS:
a practical guide to successful
growth techniques for small companies

MANAGING THE SURVIVAL OF SMALLER COMPANIES

A. C. HAZEL
and
A. S. REID

Business Books Limited   London

First published 1973

© ARTHUR CURWEN HAZEL and ALAN SCOTT REID, 1973

ISBN 0 220 66215 0

*This book has been set in 11 on 12 point Baskerville
and printed in England by Redwood Press Limited, Trowbridge, Wiltshire
for the publishers, Business Books Limited
(Registered office: 110 Fleet Street, London EC1)
Publishing offices: Mercury House, Waterloo Road, London SE1*

Made and printed in Great Britain

Contents

Part 3 THE CURE—NINE ROUTES TO A QUICK RECOVERY

Introduction

Every company is always at risk. Dangers are all around. Your company has to fight off competition, but it's precarious as a market leader. It has to survive national economic slumps, yet not get carried away too vigorously by booms. It can be bogged down by administration, but it can easily be lost through not having enough records.

Selling too little is disastrous. But so is overtrading. Industrial disputes can ruin a company—even if its own industrial relations are perfect.

For all the advantages of small companies, they are most prone to disaster.

Alarmist? We prefer to call it realistic. Everyone knows that small companies have lots of problems—the depressingly high number of bankruptcies and liquidations show how many seem to have insoluble problems.

Are they insoluble? Or are they only seen too late? Are they, in fact, ever seen at all? Compare owners' and creditors' reasons for recent batches of small company failures:

	Owner's opinion	Creditor's opinion
Business depression	68	29
Inefficient management	28	59

Insufficient capital	48	33
Adverse domestic and personal factors	35	28
Bad debt losses	30	18
Competition	38	9
Decline in assets value	32	6
Dishonesty and fraud	0	34
Excessive overhead expense	24	9

What are the causes of decline and failure? Which ones do you think your company is in greatest danger from? Would you be able to notice symptoms of decline in your company? Are you sure there aren't any there already?

And how do you stop decline once you've spotted it? What precautions can you take to prevent it getting a fatal grip? How do you pull a company back out of the doldrums and give it a stronger base?

We've written this book for all managers and owners of small businesses, whatever the present state of their company. After all, prevention is better than cure, and every liquidated company was once a going concern, even if not for long.

This is our second book - but perhaps should have been written first. It sets out to help you put your company on a solid footing - or get it back on one. We have been through the mill, made many mistakes, profited by them, and finished up with a reasonable degree of success. The book, therefore, is based on experience gained in the hard school of small business. We hope reading it will prove to be one of your profitable investments.

Our previous book, *Enjoying a profitable business*, is a guide to techniques which will help your company to grow. But successful growth needs a firm foundation.

A. C. HAZEL
A. S. REID

Part 1 SYMPTOMS AND CAUSES

If symptoms of decline stood out like beacons, more firms would recover in time. But symptoms have to be looked for—there's usually no time left if you wait for the beacons to light up.

Just 'keeping your eyes peeled' is not enough—you have to know what to look for. And you need aids. The captain of a ship certainly keeps his 'eyes peeled', but he has charts to let him know what to search for, and radar and night glasses to help him look. The manager needs to know what the dangers are, and he needs the aid of documentation and analyses.

When danger is seen, it can't be dealt with until everything is known about it. Decline can't be stopped until its causes are known, and unfortunately there are only too many things which can cause decline.

Early recognition of symptoms and an appreciation of causes are the manager's best aids in keeping away misfortune.

Chapter 1 What Signs Can You See in Your Company?

Like a ship steaming blithely off course, even a company that gives every indication of successful trading could be headed for disaster. In business, there is no room for complacency and overconfidence.

There is no point in constantly worrying yourself into an ulcer, but only when you have your finger on the pulse of every part of your company should you confidently assert that, for the present, all is well.

Early symptoms are well hidden—but they are there. A glance at Chapters 3, 4, and 5 will show you just how many things can cause decline, and you could probably add a few risks peculiar to your particular business. When any of these causes start to act on your affairs, symptoms are shown—if you know where to look.

Half the trouble, of course, is that we don't want to know bad news—we're too busy looking for new customers, increases in sales. With the result that, like a wronged husband or wife, we are the last to see something that others have suspected for ages. The advantage of being on the lookout for symptoms is that the causes can often be isolated early enough to correct them with little damage being done, or preparations made for new courses of action. And being the first to see our own weaknesses gives us a chance to strengthen them before others take advantage of us.

THE BANK STATEMENT

Bank statements can give the first warning of difficulties, especially when a firm is operating on overdraft. For apart from the meanings in the figures themselves, having an overdraft means having an expert financial adviser—the bank manager—who takes a keen interest in your affairs. To most small and medium sized companies, the ordinary high street clearing bank is always the first source of finance. If in the past they have seemed unfriendly, that image is certainly changing now, and more and more they are going to be the first and foremost suppliers of capital—venture capital as well—to small companies.

So getting a bank in as deep as you can, as early as you can, pays off in a number of ways. You get capital, advice and statements which carry much information between the lines.

Assume, for example, that you have agreed an overdraft with your bank manager, and have prepared, under his guidance perhaps, a cash flow statement. Normally an overdraft will have a limit of 10 per cent of sales turnover, though in exceptional circumstances it could go as high as 15 per cent. So if your turnover was £250,000 a year you might have an overdraft of £25,000. With a budgeted profit of 5 per cent net on sales the yearly profit would be £12,500. If the sales were at a consistent level over the year, this would mean a profit of roughly £1000 per month, and theoretically your overdraft should come down steadily and be under £13,000 by the end of the year.

Or, perhaps, your sales would be increasing (yours being a growing business) at 10 per cent per annum—£25,000. Since increased sales invariably mean increased debtors as well as higher bills, to have sufficient working capital your overdraft might go up to £27,500. Nevertheless, if your pattern of payments to your creditors remains constant, and your debtors payments also remain constant (in relation to sales) you should still be reducing the overdraft by at least £1000 per month (the monthly net profit figure).

Since such steady income rates are not that common, with nearly every product or service having some seasonal fluctuations such simple patterns will be the exception rather than the rule. But the basic principle remains the same. With a prepared cash flow, the bank statement will illustrate the figures that have to be watched—the overdraft in relation to sales.

Any increase in the overdraft which is out of line with an increase in sales means something is wrong. Perhaps your credit control is slipping, and your debtors are getting out of hand. Or perhaps you are not taking proper advantage of credit facilities from your suppliers. If seasonal fluctuations are allowed for, this discrepancy could mean that you are manufacturing for stock, or perhaps, in the case of a distributor before Christmas, acquiring for stock before a big selling season. But these fluctuations should be allowed for in your cash flow statements and budgets. And a very simple way of double checking is to keep comparing your bank statement with those of the previous year.

Relevant to the sort of business you are in and the rate of transaction, whether buying or selling, bank statements should be inspected as regularly as possible—monthly, weekly, daily even. There are no other early symptoms so simple and accurate.

THE BALANCE SHEET

Balance sheets are definitive statements about a firm's finances, so they should be expected to provide a wealth of information. And they do. Financial pundits pride themselves on being able to 'read between the lines' of balance sheets and discover the firm's past workings, present trends and future problems. A balance sheet is like a medical record, a diarist's writings, the palm of a hand to a fortune teller.

The trouble is that the balance sheet is usually not available until two months or so after the end of a company's financial year. And that might be too late. For whatever they might tell you about the future, they tell it with the finality of fact, rather than with the helpful hints of the bank statement. With these disadvantages, the best way to use balance sheets is to take those for the past five years as well and to look for trends. If the latest balance sheet shows a worryingly low profit, perhaps comparison with previous ones will disclose that expenses have been creeping up.

Noticing that something is wrong is at least a step in the right direction. Finding out exactly where the fault is, gets you that much closer to a solution. Management ratios, or business ratios, are excellent aids to detection.

MANAGEMENT RATIOS

Normally, management ratios are various items of expenses expressed as percentages or ratios of sales, though they may also express various other comparisons, such as assets and liabilities. (Some of the more common ones are shown below.) Many of the ratios can be worked out from balance sheets —other more obscure ones, and those needed more frequently, depend on figures being given in monthly reporting documents.

Like the balance sheet, business ratios on their own tell you little (if expenses were twice sales, you would know about it long before you worked out your ratios—if you even bothered to at that stage). Where they are invaluable is in showing trends, and therefore they must be constantly compared with records of the last four or five years, and also measured against budgeted performance. Ideally, too, if you become 'ratio conscious' they should be calculated frequently. (Getting someone in each department to do their own saves you trouble, and also opens their eyes.)

A straightforward EXPENSES-SALES comparison will obviously show up anything that is wrong, but isolation will take more investigating. For example, you might have budgeted for a gross margin of 30 per cent; on sales of £200,000 your gross should then be £60,000. But you find that you have lost £10,000 profit contribution. If you are only making 5 per cent on sales, this profit decline would mean that this year you would only be breaking even.

But where, and what is wrong? It could be that the gross margin of 30 per cent has slipped to 25 per cent, by taking on a higher proportion of big customers, and giving too much away in discounts. Or perhaps your product mix has changed and you are selling more and more products on which there is a low mark up, and fewer and fewer where you might have had a gross margin of 40 per cent or even more.

On the other hand your trading expenses, normally 20 per cent of sales, might have crept up to 25 per cent, and this would have exactly the same effect. Perhaps a falling market has sent you selling further and further afield with corresponding increases in sales and distribution costs. Rents might have gone up, salaries might be higher.

Keeping track of all items of expenses, expressed as percentages of sales, will pinpoint variations and help you track down lost profits. Apart from these invaluable EXPENSE RATIOS, there are a number of other ratios which illustrate symptoms of decline. What must be remembered with all of them is that it is variations in the ratios, and the trends of those variations that count, and not the figures themselves. So if you haven't worked out any of them yet, you either have to wait about a year before they mean anything worthwhile (some will change month to month, some seasonally) or you have to dig up your last five years balance sheets and control documents, and work out the ratios for those years.

The solvency of a company is easily measured by the CURRENT RATIO which indicates working capital by the surplus of current assets over current liabilities. A safe ratio, and often higher than necessary in many types of business, is 3 : 1.

Closer to the mark, and often disturbing in what it shows, is the LIQUID ASSETS RATIO, or LIQUIDITY RATIO. This is the ratio between liquid current assets, which is cash and any cash equivalent, and current liabilities. Giving too much credit, and taking too much yourself will reduce this ratio, and running close to insolvency here means there is little leeway for even minor crises. This ratio should improve as a company establishes itself and operates good credit control and is able to pay its debts on time. New companies, or ones expanding with a new product, keep a careful watch on this one.

Variations in this ratio, and the current ratio, are often preceded by a change in the DEBTORS/CREDIT SALES RATIO.

The dangers of overtrading can be predicted by the NET SALES/NET WORTH RATIO, as well as by the liquidity ratio, and it will also show up an under-utilisation of assets.

Anything to do with stock is a frequent bugbear of companies and the wrong stock situation can herald many a disaster, with too little often being as potentially harmful as too much. Dividing the sales at cost by the value of stock on stock-taking dates gives the STOCK TURNOVER—the number of times the stock has been sold over a period. A stable ratio is healthy enough, but would mean that any sales expansion would require extra financing (an upward trend would mean finance is available), while falling ratio would mean stock is piling up. And the ratio of STOCKS/WORKING CAPITAL is also important, for stocks are the least liquid of current assets. Having vast assets in stocks isn't going to help if sales are declining and you need money to pull yourself out of difficulties with, say, a new product.

Any variation in expense ratios or other ratios over a period means a change in your circumstances—hopefully for the better, but they illustrate decline just as well. Always, the reason behind the variation must be sought out, for only then can corrective action be taken.

One ratio that, at the end of the day, sums up all the activities is the RETURN ON INVESTMENT (ROI)—are you getting more or less for your money than you were last year? Calculation of the ROI can be best shown by the 'Du Pont Pyramid' (see Fig. 1).

MISLEADING FIGURES

Unfortunately you can be headed for an upset even when your bank statement shows a steady decline of overdraft and a healthy cash flow, when the balance sheets provide all the right figures, when the management ratios indicate good health in every sphere and when it is obvious you are getting a good return on your investment. For even while you are expanding you might be losing your place in the market, or be getting into the wrong position in the market.

So the market will always give the first symptoms—the market is all important. It is always said of anyone who is successful in any branch of business—from stockbroker to secondhand car dealer—that 'He knows the market'. Any businessman who does not keep a finger on the pulse of the market is bound to run out of luck, and business, very soon.

One of the beliefs in business is that you must either grow or die. But even if you are feeling proud of yourself for having

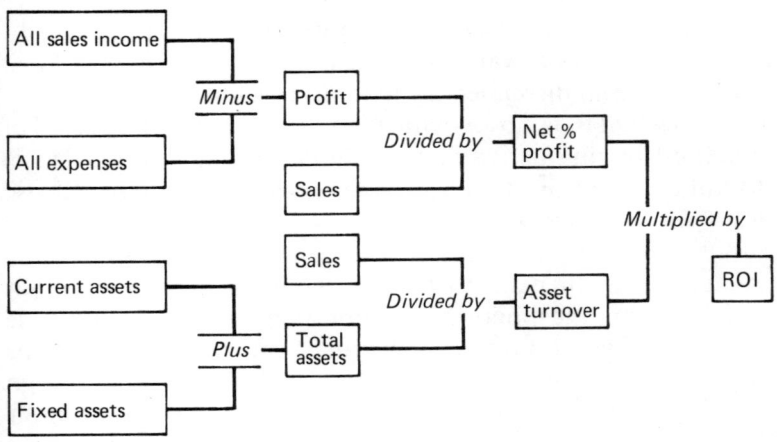

Figure 1. The 'Du Pont' pyramid

achieved a growth rate of 10 per cent a year, that is nothing to be proud of if the market is growing at 15 per cent or 20 per cent a year. Your business might be growing but your market share is declining, and that needs as much attention as if it was your business as a whole that was declining; without attention, it soon will be.

And it's not sufficient only to look at the market share either. A healthy growth rate of sales turnover, an increase of market share, perhaps even emergence as the market leader, is going to be worthless if the whole market is on a downward trend, and headed for a long steady decline. Your new position as market leader might have come about because all your competitors have been astute enough to get out while the going's good. An increasing share of a declining market does not hold many prospects.

PERSONNEL AND PERSONAL SYMPTOMS

Chairmen try to sell branches of their empires and the last people to be told are the ones included in the job lot. A company is headed for the rocks, and the last person to become aware of it is the managing director. When these are true, it is largely because we see what we want to see—or don't see what we do not want to see.

So adverse trends in management ratios, changes in product mix or changes in customer mix resulting in changes in gross margin, an upward creeping breakeven point, a setback in profits are all dismissed as 'temporary signs of an unusually early seasonal fluctuation which normally precedes a period of increased buying activity'. Even hunches that the market is declining are excused through over-anxiety and an unrealistic desire for excessive security.

But if the signs are there, *someone's* eyes are going to be open enough to see them. And then, of course, there is also that undefinable atmosphere or intuition that seems to precede fact itself. If you do not feel, or admit, this intuition, its signs in others are recognisable. Some people in the firm will resign —trying to read between the lines could lead you to discover that a higher salary (and higher than you could afford, even though you remind yourself that no-one costs more than an inferior employee, and that the most expensive man or woman could also be the cheapest) isn't the most important factor. Try to find out a bit more about the firm he is going to. If prospects there don't look that much more attractive, could it be that one of the assets your employee might find there is the security which he thinks your firm lacks? If two or three people want to leave, there must be something wrong, even if they don't tell you out straight that they think your firm is heading downhill—though you should try to encourage an atmosphere that permits open discussion of problems and anxieties. But even then, if someone only has a hunch, they may not want to risk argument on such tenuous evidence.

Others in the firm who have similar apprehensions might be more optimistic, or perhaps less adventurous, or might be faced with a job shortage in their field—so they'll stay on. But there'll be some change. A new lethargy, a difference in attitude towards you, less enthusiasm in meetings, fewer suggestions in the suggestion box, fewer actions on their own initiative. Competitors will be spoken about more frequently, and differently. 'Rumble is giving us a lot of trouble down South' will become 'Old Rumble's doing very well in the South lately'.

The trouble with these changing attitudes within the company is that cause and effect begin to get mixed up. If lethargy creeps in because people feel prospects are poor, that very lethargy will begin to make your prospects poor anyway.

The same cause and effect muddle in personnel symptoms is apparent in personal symptoms. Do you feel apathetic towards your business because it seems to be on the decline, or at least to have stopped growing—or is it grinding to a halt because you have lost your enthusiasm for it? Whichever comes first, such moods are indicative that the future of the firm is unlikely to be bright. Old age is, of course, a symptom of decline, for it is difficult, after life-long work, to keep up the relentless energy required to keep a company expanding. Many do manage to 'stay in the saddle' to remarkable ages, but often because they have got someone far younger working with them. Then the combination of youthful energy and enthusiasm combines with long experience to form a powerful management asset.

Personal and personnel symptoms manifest themselves first in human terms—changed atmosphere, hunches, a worsening mood. What causes these symptoms needs to be hunted down with the same urgency as that indicated by any other symptom. Left alone, the symptoms will soon show themselves in many other, less subtle ways. And all along the causes might have nothing at all to do with personal or staff problems. Their solution could prevent a whole dam of new causes of decline from building up.

Chapter 2 Tell-tale Signs That Outsiders Look For

External symptoms are the give away if you are looking for signs of decline in competitors or in other companies. But they apply equally to your own company, for someone is always on the lookout for symptoms shown by your firm.

There is not likely to be any one symptom that reliably proclaims to outsiders that a firm is in decline, though when an announcement of regret is made, there is no shortage of people who nod wisely and say 'Could see it coming from miles away —had to happen'. Sometimes it can be seen before the last hasty slide arrives, but only by reading a number of signs. Even so, the system is not infallible, Rolls-Royce being an excellent example of that. Here are some symptoms to look out for and put together.

SALES ACTIVITY

No good businessman ignores his competitors for long, for without keeping a careful eye on them, they are going to do something that will upset all his plans. The easiest way of keeping tabs is to watch the other firm's sales activity, and most companies require their salesmen to report on competitive action. Managers and owners scan papers and magazines as carefully for their competitors' names as they do for their own, and advertisements get as close a scrutiny as do editorials These practices lead to a heightened sensitivity to any change in the tempo of competitors' sales activity.

A competitor's every move should be thought about and analysed, for first reactions are likely to be false. Obviously news about new products, or advertisements for them, or about new areas covered, which all seems to be part of a continuing pattern of expansion, is straight-forward stuff unlikely to cause anything other than anxiety to the outside watcher.

But flurries of activity which seem incongruous or illogical should be looked at for their hidden meaning. Is the sudden cutting of costs to what, by your calculations, is an unprofitable level, a stock clearing move heralding a new line—or a desperate gamble? Why has he taken on two more salesmen in an area where one seemed to be doing an adequate job—can there be enough genuine business there, or is it a short-term move to squeeze something, anything, out of a flagging market? Do his new crop of advertisements say or promise anything new, or are they anxiously flogging a dead horse? Does any of the new activity anticipate (for you) good or bad news?

The answer is unlikely to be either clear or immediate—but further symptoms may help.

COMPETITORS' STAFF

Short of an obliging defector who comes to you and spills the beans that a competitor is headed for disaster, there is much that can be gathered from what his staff are up to. Some firms periodically run ads for imaginary positions in their own firms to see if they get any applicants from competitors, and interview them to see what they can sift. Depending on your degree of dedication to succeed, the ethics of this are questionable (these firms are also likely to be the ones who run anonymous ads to check on the loyalty of their own staff, which is an even more dubious move). But from time to time you do advertise for genuine positions and simply the fact that a number of the applicants come from one competitor is an indication that not everyone there is happy. And there is no harm in taking advantage of information freely given at interviews.

The job ads pages in papers are useful in another way, for they tell you what changes are going on in other firms. An ad for a new position means a new department or expansion, but sometimes some firms seem to be constantly advertising for similar jobs. They can't all be for expansion, even on the level of junior salesmen, and a high turnover indicates dissatisfaction. When the jobs advertised are managerial —perhaps for the same managerial post three or four times in as many years—the indications are that much more forceful. A specialist engineering company in the Midlands recently went through three managing directors in only about 18 months—signs of desperately trying to put right the financial mess they soon disclosed they were in. This type of trouble spotting is made more difficult by the growing tendency for anonymous job ads or those handled through agencies and consultants. But to have some pulling power, the ads must give a fair amount of detail, and people in the relevant type of business can usually, by elimination, be pretty certain of the advertiser's identity.

Of course, even if you correctly diagnose extensive difficulties from the nature of staff movements at your competitors, it might only be a temporary setback, and you should look for some secondary symptoms.

OUTSIDE APPEARANCES

Nearly all detection work involves looking for something different, or unusual patterns of behaviour, something that doesn't 'belong'. In business it is the same. Your management ratios are clues to something good or bad only when they change. A change of atmosphere is a clue that should be followed up. And if there is nothing to look for in a competitor's activities, there is unlikely to be any change in the first place to prompt you to look.

So if your competitor has always had premises that look as if they could do with a coat of paint, the very shabbiness of the place doesn't necessarily mean that things are going badly for him. But for another, when pressures begin to bite one of the first costs cut back is maintenance. The yearly coat of paint will be missed, vehicles will begin to look older, less well kept. Perhaps you will hear that machinery is being patched and kept going when it should obviously be replaced.

Other signs might be there. The receptionist in the smart entrance hall disappears (with the pot plants), and a bell and a two way speaker to the switchboard operator take her place. The firm's embossed two colour letterheads give way to single colour printed. Their glossy brochures turn matt and lose two pages, their Christmas dance gives way to a quick cocktail party, or simply a card from the managing director. Regular ads and expensive calendars disappear.

Sadly, since many competitors during working hours are quite friendly outside hours, yours is at fewer and fewer meetings—and always seems to leave straight afterwards, his cheerful countenance replaced by a preoccupied frown.

No-one likes to see someone go out of business, and more often than not when a competitor has his back to the wall it is because of something that threatens that whole market, or more widespread economic pressures that affect everyone. As likely as not, you will be up against it as well.

But an expanding company, or an able executive anxious to set out on his own or do a rescue operation on a failing company, is always on the lookout for a potential buy. Having found the type of company and decided on an area, these symptoms, and one day, the up-to-date trading records at Company House, will help in making the choice of which company to approach with an offer.

If you see none of these symptoms in your own company, you are fortunate. But there is no room for complacency.

No one is likely to ever believe his company is inviolable, but it is all to easy to presume there are only one or two things which can threaten your company. Unfortunately there are a lot more.

Some causes are beyond your control, and it is simply bad luck to be hit by them. Some cannot solely be put at the hands of Fate—you would have to share some of the blame. Others have no excuse.

Which threaten your business most?

Chapter 3 It Can Happen to You—
But Don't Blame Yourself

(See Part 2, Chapter 6)

CATASTROPHES AND DISASTERS

There are all too many of these, from the frequent FIRES and FLOODS to the more exotic RIOTS, SONIC BOOMS, EARTHQUAKES, TREMORS and FRAUDS. Everything can be insured against, but there is more to it than covering possible loss or damage.

You've spent years building up your business, with a select band of customers. Then a fire ruins part of your machine shop, or a gale blows part of your roof off and a flood soaks everything in your warehouse. It could be the end of your business. Your customers have their own worries; missed deliveries and unfinished products are going to upset their plans too. You can't blame them for going elsewhere while you are recovering—or for staying away even when you are back in business. Nor can you blame your competitors for taking advantage of your incapacity.

Perhaps there will be no work for many of your staff until you get going again—it could take ages to build the right team up again. You might have to wait ages for replacement plant, or for alternative premises whether new or temporary.

If you are on a smallholding with five acres of greenhouses, a sonic boom might mean more than a bonanza for the local glazier. It could mean ruined crops, a delay for a new growing period. Again, lost customers.

With catastrophes, it is not so much the actual destruction

that finishes off a company, but the difficulty in getting back into the position it was in before it all took place.

ECONOMIC AND GOVERNMENT CHANGES

If you are only just scraping through, a sudden squeeze by the Government can plunge you forever into the red. A massive new tax could be put on your product—as happened many years ago when 100 per cent purchase tax was put on various electrical appliances. SET put paid to many small businesses. Abolishing various grants and subsidies threaten many firms that rely on them. The Industrial Training Act helped the birth of many consultancies, seminar and course organisers. Abolish the Act, and some are bound to flounder.

Changes in tariffs or currency exchange rates can badly hit exporters and importers. Changes in the bank rate, in hire purchase and hire conditions can have great effect. Hundreds of small firms start up, expand and flourish when a Government sets off a boom. It would do them well if they spent a few minutes each Monday remembering what it was that got them going. If a set of conditions can set a chain of events in motion, removing those conditions is usually going to snap that chain in many places.

Remember—easy come, easy go.

LOCALISED DEPRESSIONS

Government action can produce unemployment which usually has a very serious effect in certain regions, though it may not be so serious across the whole country. The result is that small companies in the area can suddenly find themselves with a marked reduction in sales. For example in the West Midlands during the period 1971/72 there was a very substantial increase in unemployment, and in short time working.

This was a region which had formerly been very prosperous, almost the most prosperous due to the rapid growth of the motor car and engineering markets. Suddenly this region, which had not experienced depression before, was taken by surprise by the localised depression, and this made everyone extremely nervous about spending money. So much so that a large number of small manufacturers who made parts for the large manufacturers had to close down, and this in turn affected local shop keepers who also went out of business. In addition there were many bankruptcies, and the bad debts, of course, affected other companies within the region with a snowballing effect.

GEOGRAPHIC CHANGES

A motorway or a bypass can turn an old established, busy, and profitable garage into a deserted liability with rusty pumps standing in silent testimony to past complacency. A restaurant could suffer as quickly. New no-parking laws and the creation of one way streets can turn busy shopping streets into fast thoroughfares, or areas which are only reached with difficulty after a dozen other shops have been passed.

A new housing estate with a comprehensive shopping area could ruin the prospects of a nearby general dealer which has served the area for ages. Rezoning could force a move, and the loss of established trade. Even the resiting of an airport can seriously affect small businesses.

INDUSTRIAL ACTION

It is rare for a small company to get into difficulties from all its own workers striking against it. Small companies stand a much better chance of having peaceful industrial relations. But they are still very vulnerable to industrial action, even if they don't lift a finger to cause it.

A national strike by members of one union will involve every firm that has members on its payroll—and while small firms have a high proportion of non-union employees, the repercussions still travel strongly to the most unexpected places. Perhaps coal cannot be delivered, parts cannot be sent off, orders stop coming in as bigger customers' reserves pile up. It is unfortunate that small companies never start any large scale strike—but they suffer the most when there is one.

DEATH AND DOMESTIC CRISES

The sudden and unexpected death of a firm's managing director or owner, or of a partner, can easily spell the death of the company too. Small companies don't have the padding of large companies which can absorb such upheavals. Everything happens too rapidly, effects are felt instantly, there is no-one to take over at a moment's notice, with a long reshuffle conveniently taking place lower and lower down in the hierarchy. There can be added complications if it is a major shareholder who dies – death duties might only be payable by selling the company altogether, for if the death is unexpected, perhaps in a motor accident, not enough steps might have been taken (or could have been taken) to avoid crippling estate duty.

Serious illness, too, can have terminating effects – the long absence and uncertainty for the future when a key person in the firm is taken ill is not easily got over, especially, perhaps, if much of the firm's business has relied on that person's close contacts with customers. And anything which detracts effort for some period can have equal effect, if it concerns a really key person—the strains of a divorce, illness in the family or other family problems. The day to day success of a small company depends almost entirely on the driving force and enthusiasm which comes from the top. Take that away, and the lethargy spreads rapidly.

Although some steps can be taken to mitigate the effects of these causes (see Part 2, Chapter 6), some effect is unavoidable, and it is frequently serious. If there is a possibility of some control over ramifications, the causes themselves are beyond human control. In the next chapter, the blame is not so easily put on Fate's shoulders, or on other peoples'.

Chapter 4 Perhaps it Could be Partly Your Fault

(See Part 2, Chapter 7)

BAD DEBT LOSSES

For years and years you've traded mostly with one large, seemingly stable company, growing as the giant grew, making little effort to spread your net. After all, why spend money selling to reluctant buyers when one company gladly takes nearly all your output. Suddenly you read that your customer has gone into liquidation in these days, nobody should say of any company 'They're as safe as a house') and your accountant tells you that they owe you £135,000. (It's a big amount to let a debtor build up to, but not unusual for an old customer and a large, respected one.)

It's not your fault if one of your customers goes bust—but it is your fault if he owes you more than you can afford to lose without going bust yourself.

LARGE-SCALE COMPETITION

Small companies are far greater innovators than large companies. Therein lies the success of many, and the death of many. Too often a small company pioneers a new product, a new process, does the research and planning, sweats through proving and the launch, does it all well on a modest scale. Then the big boys move in, skirting patents if necessary, and steamroll the small company into obscurity. Even rights payments can be only a form of compensation if they also mean the end of the familiar life of the company, and of its very reason for existence.

INDUSTRIAL ACTION

Occasionally, of course, direct industrial action is taken against a small company, and difficulties cannot be blamed on someone else. While owners and managers in these firms should be accustomed to getting together with the representatives of the workers to sort out grievances, there can be occasions when there seems to be no solution at all. Usually this would be where, in a highly competitive business, wages simply cannot be increased since a price increase would lose too many sales.

But such examples of straightforward arithmetic can often also break a deadlock—provided everything is open and above board. Few people really want to jeopardise their own jobs, and an open approach and free discussion about every possible alternative is likely to find some solution—a product improvement to justify higher selling price, increased productivity, greater sales coverage, etc.

THE UNEASE OF LOW GROSS MARGINS

In businesses with high break-even points, notably in wholesaling, companies can move rapidly from good profits to disastrous losses. For example, in some trades a wholesaler may have a gross margin of 19 per cent, but his net profit on sales might only be 2 per cent—in food distribution the gross margin may be as little as 9 per cent and the net profit on sales even lower than 1 per cent. And with many of the expenses fixed, such as premises, cash tied up in stock, transport, excessive debits, it can mean that 10 months of the year go by before break-even is reached.

Under these circumstances a company has only to lose one or two good customers—perhaps through mergers or takeovers—which in the past contributed a tenth of sales, say £100,000, for profits to dwindle to next to nothing. And there's little that can be done about it suddenly—a cut-back in wages, or running down stock takes time.

When the loss of a tenth of sales can mean the loss of a complete business, the anxiety of low gross margins highlights other risk areas. Even pilfering or theft—especially if dealing in low-quantity, high-cost items—can cripple a company. And as with fire or flood, insurance payouts can often still not prevent losing invaluable customers during delays in deliveries.

DECLINE IN ASSETS VALUE

Just as 'geographic' changes can whisk away sales—as mentioned in Chapter 3—similar changes can leave you, still with customers, but with a rapidly decreasing value on your property. Lack of foresight, not enough attention to likely developments, and the long-standing, solid figure of assets could start to shrink.

Financial assets—shares, holdings abroad, investments —can be changed by economic fluctuations, or by the falling fortunes of other companies.

It is not only falling sales turnover that can cause misfortune—assets form an important part of the balance sheets, and their rise, or stability at least, is vital.

LOSS OF AGENCY OR FRANCHISE

Some franchises are so coveted, so dependable, that getting one seems like getting a licence to print money—though invariably the better the franchise, the more stringent the qualifications necessary for it. But if having the advantages of a big company name and prestige, with its advertising, accounting and purchasing power behind you, makes agency and franchise life attractive, part of the price you pay is lack of complete independence. So even when things are going well, you can't be sure what will happen at the end of your current contract period.

Divisions of area, logical when agreements were drawn up, may seem inhibiting to the franchiser ten years later when, perhaps, new industrial sites or housing estates, new lines of communication have sprung up. Or even if your operation has been profitable, a number of the remaining franchises may have been slipping into the red, and the whole operation could be closed down. Whether it then means the end of your whole business or not depends on your ability to keep the customers you have built up, and to use your reputation in a slightly different direction.

SHORTAGE OF KEY MATERIALS

You can hardly be held responsible if civil wars in distant lands, or international squabbles result in dwindling supplies and rapidly rising prices of the main material in the products you manufacture or distribute. But if you know of no other substance that could do almost equally well, or have no other products to change to, and have no contingency plans at all, then you are likely to get little sympathy.

A salesman must know his product, a carpenter his wood. An owner of a furniture factory should know both, and keep an active interest in the origins of his key materials. Where the materials come from, how they are extracted, refined or processed, what the reserve resources are, where there are alternative sources (and what their costs are)— these are all things you should know about the materials in your products.

FRAUD

The day after you wonder why your accountant hasn't phoned to say why he is not at the office, a letter from the taxmen, or from your largest supplier about some discrepancies in cheques and invoices, sends a chill up your spine. While your trusted accountant of fifteen years service, or the salesmanager who suddenly seemed to have found the formula for moving your products, sits in the Mediterranean sun, you watch everything crumble around you as you pay off debts you never knew you had.

In some cases you definitely cannot be blamed. Some dodges and fiddles are so polished that they are only discovered after years, and then often only by luck. Even then, or even when something fishy is suspected, it can take a team of experts months to work out exactly what has been done. Too

27

often though, an airy dismissal of figure work 'I never could understand all that. *You* see to it' and the attitude that it is only manufacturing, selling, and profits that matter in a company, breed exactly the right conditions for any crime —opportunity and motivation.

Less often, and more embarrassing (perhaps it happens more than is admitted) you plunge into what looks like the golden opportunity for success, offered by some kindly man who called on you, recommended by a friend of a friend. If something looks too good to be true, it usually is. People have 'bought', for ridiculously low prices, the Eiffel Tower, the Golden Gate bridge, assorted ocean liners, buried treasure, titanium mines, exclusive rights to tomorrow's miracle fabric, etc., etc. And it could happen to you—the best salesmen, the most enthusiastic business-men are often the most gullible buyers, the least cautious when 'opportunity' presents itself. Like racehorses, the mouths of gift horses bear looking into.

MACHINERY BREAKDOWN

So many activities in small companies are 'one-man bands'. There's rarely room or work for assistants and deputies, and everyone's role becomes just that much more exclusive and responsible than it would be in a large company. The same can be said of machinery and equipment—careful costing ensures that machines are utilised to the maximum, so a major breakdown could be disastrous. Especially so if it was a machine that played a major automated role in a production process. You can't be expected to have a reserve on standby, but favourable parts supplies, service guarantees, and machine loan facilities could prevent a destructive layoff.

INSUFFICIENT CAPITAL

It is not only new companies that knock at the doors of the banks and other sources of finance, asking for venture capital. Expansion, new plant, development of new products and new markets—these all cost a lot of money, money that is tied up in stock, buildings, credit to customers and so on.

Normally, since it is easier to get growth capital than venture capital, small companies make sure of getting it before plans are made, and time their moves accordingly. Usually, if a minor squeeze is on, it won't make much difference if expansion plans have to be delayed for a few months.

But suppose a competitor enters your market offering an improved product, or a lower price, which you can only match by design changes, greater automation, or higher production runs giving lower unit costs. If you haven't got, and can't get hold of the capital needed to finance the necessary changes, you could easily be left high and dry.

GROWTH IN SIZE

It seems strange to suspect company growth of being responsible for company decline—but it can happen in a number of ways. Perhaps the most frequent is through overtrading. In the exuberance of early success every order that comes along is accepted and delivery dates promised. Suddenly more and more has to be spent on materials, and debts mount. At the same time more workers have to be taken on and your overdraft stretches even further to pay wages. Then your creditors start demanding payment and you are still manufacturing for the enticing orders that came in a while ago. While desperately holding back your creditors with one hand, you are trying with the other to persuade your first customers to pay —except that they are perhaps in the same situation as you, and are going to pay as late as they possibly can. Then you have to start cancelling orders because your suppliers won't let you have any more materials on credit. Some money comes in, but goes straight out again. The excitement of a success beyond your wildest expectations turns into the failure you always dreaded.

But even if your growth is carefully planned and the excesses of overtrading are avoided, growth still holds some menace. The success of many small companies depends not so much on a particular virtue of their product, but on the method of operation of the firm, its attitude to both customers and supliers, and its high productivity—from managing director down through every activity—resulting from a collective enthusiasm.

Growth brings changes, and there are dangers in changes. All at once there is no time for the friendly meetings with suppliers, and customers who had pleasant reminders about overdue accounts now get printed notes and red stickers. The switchboard seems to become de-personalised. Workers with worries find there is no-one to listen to them, and grievances can no longer be talked over with the managing director. New forms, rules and regulations are introduced. The small firm has become a medium sized firm, with large aspirations. Everyone has retreated behind glass, paper, and desks. The driving spirit vanishes, productivity falls, the unit cost gets higher and higher, debtors take longer, creditors seem impatient.

Ambition and success too easily conceal misadventure.

TWILIGHT YEARS

Companies are often compared to people—they have personalities, characters, even changing moods. For many laws they are even considered as people, and can, for instance, sue or be sued. And like people they can grow old and tired. Usually this happens when the people in it are growing old and tired too—or at least the key people are. It need not only be that a product is not changed to keep pace with changing demands, but this itself does often happen.

Somehow, a general malaise creeps into everything. Marketing loses its dynamism through familiarity and boredom. Procrastination takes over in administration, quality control in production seems to become less demanding. Everyone, from the old managing director down feels a lack of challenge and excitement, and second best becomes good enough, with 9.40 a.m. being accepted for 9.30. It doesn't take long for customers and competitors to sense this, and with the reflection that 'Old Smith has gone on too long', they press ahead and leave Old Smith's company to dwindle out its days (see Part 2, Chapter 7).

As mentioned before, no-one likes to admit their mistakes,

and it would be comforting to include a lot more causes for decline in this and the previous chapter, and to go on now to Prevention and Cure. But that would be fostering self-delusion. In the next Chapter there are some frequent causes of company decline where the fault is almost entirely within the company—the only consolation is found in such comforting sayings as 'People will be people' and 'No-one's perfect'.

Chapter 5 You've No-one to Blame But Yourself

(See Part 2, Chapter 8)

HIGH AND CHANGING BREAK-EVEN

While sales turnover increases every year as a company sells more and more of its product, behind the scenes it could be getting into an increasingly precarious position. A creeping break-even point is a common cause of profits being turned into losses. Wages increase, the price of materials goes up marginally and the unit cost climbs steadily. Naturally you won't be completely unaware of this, but often the care that went into establishing the selling price of the product when it was launched, is not repeated by all costs being regularly reviewed.

Even when you are sure that your price increases have kept your gross margin at 30 per cent, and it has not slipped down to 25 per cent, it could be that in the changed circumstances of the current market a 30 per cent gross margin gives you too high a break-even point for comfort. The chart in Fig. 2 shows the effect of three prices, giving different gross margins, on the break-even point of a product.

A high break-even point might have been suitable when there was little competition and the market was safe, with a long growth potential. But increasing costs, fiercer competition and the possibility of market saturation could make a high break-even disastrous. Again, sudden rises for materials costs, or of the wages bill,

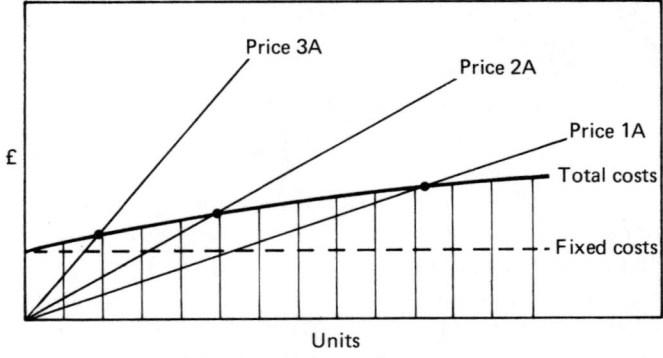

Figure 2. Higher prices (therefore higher gross margins) lower the break-even points.

could mean the high break-even causes a high loss.

MARKET DOMINATION

Although every businessman goes about his work determined to 'capture the market', once he has he finds the position of captor precarious. If a company has, say, a 75 per cent share of the market, practically the only way it can increase its sales is by constantly expanding the market itself—a task which gets progressively more difficult.

A newcomer, however, attracted by the pickings of a thriving market, will find it childishly easy to get a small share. Soon this company might have 10 per cent of the market. Increasing that to 15 per cent is still going to prove a much easier exercise than the dominator will find hanging onto its 75 per cent to be. The market dominator will find itself cutting its selling price, spending more on advertising—its break-even point will get higher and higher, while its sales forecasts will look more and more dubious. And if this product is the one that brings in 70 per cent of the firm's revenue, it is very easy for a serious decline to set in.

TOO LITTLE DIVERSIFICATION

The market dominator above, instead of walking a tightrope with his competitors busy shaking it, would be on far steadier

33

a footing if his product which had cornered the market was only one of a dozen in his range, and which contributed only 20 per cent, instead of 70 per cent, to the annual turnover. Many, many causes of decline are directly or indirectly due to having too many eggs in one basket. The reliance on a single product leaves a company vulnerable to far too many ill winds —competitive action, fall in demand, shortage or rise in the price of raw materials, tax and tariff changes. A company with a single product is like a restaurant which constantly has only one item on the menu.

Only slightly better is the company which has a number of products, but all linked to the same market—extras for cars perhaps, with no accessories which can be subcontracted to the major manufacturers. Such items are likely to have seasonal selling patterns, and a reduced demand at one high season would be serious. With one product, one market, or one season providing you with virtually all your turnover, it only takes one downward trend to put you firmly in the red.

The toy car industry and different branches of the clothing industry have recently shown what happens when markets change.

CHANGING MARKETS AND MATERIALS

No-one really knows what tomorrow will bring, but many people place their whole livelihood on their own projections. The most adamant are usually those that believe that tomorrow will always be the same as today, and that people will behave then as they do now. So when tomorrow turns out to be different, and people are asking for different things, they are left stranded.

Many small builders, plumbers, and other tradesmen and merchants would be better off if they worked with the DIY boom instead of trying to pretend it wasn't there. Manufacturers of cast iron rainwater products—gutters and so on —failed to see the potential when various types of plastics came onto the market, and got left out of the market. They were too caught up with tradition and materials, and seemed to ignore the market and products. Cast iron also gets left behind with baths—steel and plastic again, are that much lighter, have better, if different strength qualities, plastics can have all those shapes . . . and yet, in both ranges it has not been rainwater products or bath manufacturers who have supplied the newest, most up to date products, but firms using the new materials to make other products who have seen the enormous scope for new materials.

The cast iron believers, of course, could do well by similarly looking for different products. It is a matter of deciding whether certain products, using the best materials, are going to be your forté, or any products using a certain material. Either way, falling behind in looking for market changes and new opportunities is going to send your firm tumbling.

INVESTMENT IN SPECIALIST PLANT

Like the firm that relies too heavily on too few products or too narrow a market, the firm that relies for its production on highly specialised plant and equipment reduces its chances of survival in times of crisis. If the bottom drops out of the market you are in and you have to switch to some radically different activity, it is likely that you will have considerable difficulty in using the plant, or in selling off unwanted equipment and machinery. A heavy investment in out-of-the-ordinary plant, buildings, or even activities, such as a rare and specialised sales team, reduces a company's versatility and therefore, its ability to weather a storm.

MACHINE UTILISATION AND FIXED-PRICE CONTRACTS

Most small manufacturers have a variety of presses or moulds and they produce a range of parts, usually for other manufacturers. Unless the load on these machines is maintained for as far ahead as possible, trouble can ensue. This means that a small manufacturer should have almost continuously before him a complete picture of the future load on each machine. Thus when he is estimating against enquiries he will always bear in mind what spare capacity is available, and rather than have a machine idle, he will quote keenly on those contracts which will enable him to utilise the full capacity of a machine.

In this connection during periods of inflation small manufacturers have got themselves into great difficulty through quoting fixed prices for long runs covering lengthy periods. The Managing Director of a small manufacturing business should personally approve every quotation sent out because mistakes in this field can make or mar a business.

MARKET SATURATION

For any non-essential product, there is a saturation point beyond which you can only expect slow sales, which are replacements, or as 'new' people arrive on the scene. Even with common foodstuffs, a stage is reached when increases are governed only by population increases, and where substantial fluctuations in the positions of competing companies are rare. Still, growing along with natural market growth can be profitable enough, if enough of the population is using your product.

In sunnier climes than Britain's, recent breakthroughs in swimming bath construction methods suddenly took them out of the luxury class, and no self-respecting houseowner with enough ground to put one on would be without a swimming bath. Five or six market leaders suddenly sprang up, along with a host of others, and a lot of subsidiary linked companies, such as filtration plant manufacturers. It was only a few years, however, before saturation point was reached, and natural growth was not enough to support all the companies which had been enjoying such a bonanza. Two or three at the top survived, many crashed through trying to keep going long after all the signs of doom were there. Even the survivors kept going, not solely by their expertise and reputation specifically in swimming bath construction, but also because they were quick enough to discover other uses for the specialised and expensive equipment and labour they had invested so heavily in.

RELIANCE ON TOO FEW CUSTOMERS

Another 'all the eggs in one basket' risk. There is something comforting in having an order book filled regularly by only two or three satisfied clients. You know what they want, they order well in advance and let you know approximately what their needs will be for ages to come. Not only that, but your bank manager knows that at least *those* cheques will be coming in.

Then one day one of those customers—perhaps two, for it's quite likely they will be in similar fields—goes bust. Or they get taken over and buying is centralised. Or perhaps that particular segment of the market tails off, and the component part you have been supplying is no longer needed. Straightway you can lose easily a third of your sales.

Having only a few customers puts a firm in the same risk position as having only a few products.

USING TOO FEW SUPPLIERS

Excessive zeal in rationalising your purchasing often does more harm than good. Granted you can get good discounts and favourable credit terms if you are a major buyer of long standing. But then you base your gross margin on these low costs and if take-overs or liquidations force you to go elsewhere, your purchasing bill shoots up and your whole price structure and sales platform collapses. One of the joys of a small company is its independence—a quality that should be preserved in all things.

LACK OF EXPANSION PLANS

Being caught unprepared when your market is crying out for your product is the most frustrating way of getting into difficulties. Usually a company over-reacts, begins to gear up too rapidly and finds itself producing for the customers that were there six months ago—only now there are three new competitors as well, and it is left with a pile of stock. Or administration cannot cope, and things get in a mess through panic measures.

Contingency plans should take care of these needs, but a less obvious danger is in costing. Initial costs are worked out on existing overheads—a factory and machinery that is perhaps already paid for. But expansion is likely to mean bigger premises, more plant—new expenses that will shoot up the break-even point.

Lack of planning of any sort, in fact, is likely to send a firm on the rapid downward path—no plans for action if things go badly will make them worse. No long-term plans make short-term planning and budgeting next to impossible.

INSUFFICIENT CONTROLS AND FIGURE BLINDNESS

Paperwork is often the enemy of efficiency, and small firms are pleasantly free of it—that of their own making at any rate. But ignoring it altogether, or doing it later than should be invites trouble. Monthly reporting documents, especially, are vital. With no figures coming in, not only is the business going to slide through lack of knowledge and missed opportunities, but the downward trend won't even be noticed until it is too late.

What documents are kept up to date must be the right ones and read correctly. It's not enough to know only that turnover is increasing—what about costs, and is the gross margin constant?

NOT SEEING THE WHOLE MARKET

In the euphoria of increasing sales, many faults can be overlooked. The most common is when over-all sales are climbing, but your market share is in fact declining. If the signs given out by your competitors are ignored or not searched for, it is all too easy for them to creep up and then overtake you. When a company's sales of £300,000 represent 25 per cent of the market, and its sales are boosted to £380,000, while the market has increased so that this represents only 21 per cent of the market, then the company is really losing ground.

WRONG DECISIONS IN BAD TIMES

In the ups and downs of any country's economy there are bound to be times when everything slows down. With expensive plant and labour to be utilised, everyone invariably begins to produce for stock—which is why booms following slumps take a while to be felt all down the line. But making for stock too long, and holding too long onto labour by trying to keep your own boom time conditions going, is a sure way to book your own slump too.

EXCESSIVE CREDIT AND BAD DEBTS

Especially in the early stages of a firm or a product, the temptation is to give good credit terms—the emphasis at such times is on making sales. Such faith in human nature (or in the nature of other companies) is dangerously naive. There is in any case something suspicious about a customer who is excessively keen on long credit terms—suspicion that is all too often warranted. Too much fortune 'on paper' convinces no-one after a while, and creditors will begin to wonder what it is about your product or service that makes it necessary to sell it on such sacrificial terms.

LACK OF PROPER INSURANCE COVER

In Chapter 3 most of the catastrophes could have their effects negated, to some extent at least, by insurance. So while the disaster itself cannot be held to be your responsibility, if it turns into a complete catastrophe because you do not have insurance, that is no-one's fault but your own. Even people who conscientiously take out insurance can be caught out because their cover is not full enough, and leaves out loss of profits, cost of alternative accommodation, etc.

ADVERSE PERSONAL FACTORS

We all have failings and imperfections, but the seven most common symptoms of executive failure which in small companies usually herald company failure, have been listed as the following:

1 Lacking in human relations.
2 Inability to solve problems.
3 Immaturity.
4 Failure to delegate.

5 Inability to communicate.
6 Lack of drive.
7 Anxiety.

COMPETITOR'S ADVANTAGE ON PRODUCT OR PRICE

Market leaders, or old and well established suppliers and manufacturers, easily become complacent. What was good enough last year is good enough this year. They rely on a product or a company name having a constant appeal.

It is all too easy to lose all this to a competitor who recognises changing moods in the public, the appeal of something new, even the frequent resistance to something that *is* well established, a habit especially of new generations. A competitor, too, might be quick to see advantages in new manufacturing techniques which have become possible through new machinery, materials or skills. These could produce better products, or products at a lower price.

It is worth remembering that small companies have a better record of innovation in products and techniques than the safe-playing and slow-moving big companies. So market leaders, strong in size, financial resources and advertising expenditure, are still vulnerable. That they are is their own fault—with their resources they should be leaders in development, but it is only the few, like Pilkingtons, that are.

Luck, of course, plays a big part. Not every product designer or production manager can be equal. But if you can't be lucky in that choice and keep one step ahead, you can at least be prepared for rapid changes and be the first to follow.

EXCESSIVE OVERHEADS

Earlier, we saw how a small company can lose its character and advantages when it grows into a medium or large company. Often that cannot be avoided, and the only alternative is to stay small but effective. But there is another danger in growing too quickly, and that is that overheads increase too quickly. It happens too easily, and sometimes instead of an ideal curve of growth, the graph has to go up in steps.

The smaller the company is at starting point, the more likely this is to happen. A 'one man band' gets to the stage when paper work slows down productivity and someone has to be brought in to manage the clerical side. At the same time another salesman is needed, and a copy typist. Overnight the strength of the company has perhaps doubled, the wages bill increased by 70 per cent, and new office furniture and a typewriter have been bought. Overheads have rocketed, the break-even point has been sent soaring, and a whole campaign based on a certain product price has tumbled.

EXCESSIVE ADVERTISING EXPENDITURE

In a do-or-die gesture, many companies commit suicide by spending too much on advertising. Even for a big company, making an impact with a strong advertising campaign is a risky business, but even there they are careful not to spend more than they know they can afford even if it flops altogether. (The amount they might have spent on manufacturing for stock in anticipation of the campaign's success is a different matter, and potentially even more disastrous.)

For a small company, making a massive impact in a campaign is too nervewracking. A new product launch to consumers can easily cost up to £30,000. Doing national advertising without first arranging national distribution is going to be disastrous—especially if the campaign is a great success. Setting up national distribution and then having the campaign fizzle out will be equally disastrous. Any advertising expenditure of more than half your net earnings is gambling with the dice loaded against you. (See Part 2, Chapter 8).

Dwelling on possible misfortune is depressing, and it makes little difference whether you are responsible for the misfortune or not. But just as every cause has a symptom, and vice versa, so every cause has a remedy—well, nearly every one.

Even better than cures though, is prevention.

Part 2 PREVENTION AND CURE

Knowing what can cause a firm to decline means that you can take steps to prevent it happening—or at least to soften the blow when you are unable to prevent it. The hints on prevention which follow therefore tie up with the causes in Chapters 3, 4 and 5. Sometimes they will help to prevent the fault itself, sometimes all that can be hoped for is to make the effect less drastic.

But sometimes there is virtually no point in trying to take steps to prevent or cure a malady which is, sooner or later, inevitable. You have to decide whether the costs of prevention are not more than the costs of giving up altogether and going in for something different. Often the best thing to do is to sell up. A declining market, a powerful new competitor (a big company crowding in), some catastrophe, your own age and personal circumstances or a general discontent with that particular type of business—all these could speak loudly in favour of packing it up and doing something different.

If causes have taken effect and you do decide to cure your firm, that there is much to salvage, you also should decide whether you are going to carry out the saving operation on your own, or whether you are going to get someone in to help you—on the staff perhaps, or outside consultants. Or perhaps the best, maybe the only way is to merge with, or into, a larger company which will have the resources you need. If you do want to cure your company you might have to sacrifice some independence, so that has to be taken into account as well.

Chapter 6　Softening the Blow of Unavoidable Causes

(See Part 1, Chapter 3)

The very title of Chapter 3 suggests that there is nothing that can be done to prevent their happening, and certainly you have no control over the events themselves. To some degree though, you have control over how much they affect you, and there are doubtless some measures which could be taken which would give you almost complete protection—but at a financial (and mental) cost which is bound to be crippling.

CATASTROPHES AND DISASTERS

These can happen anytime to anyone, so:

Do insure—and take into account not only costs of buildings and equipment, but loss of business, profits and goodwill. Relate the insurance to the length of time it will take before you can start trading again, and before you can reach former levels. Consider the cost of renting equivalent premises, or of building again from scratch, so relate property to present levels.

Do get the advice of the local fire brigade in taking precautions against fire—it is difficult to be too anxious over this hazard. And do take and stick to the precautions. Keep sections such as welding well away from, say, the paint room, and be especially careful in following manufacturers' standards for storage.

Do make sure everyone shuts their doors and windows (internal windows too) every night.

Do have a good safe in which important records and money is locked every night.

Do take local conditions into account, especially abroad. There could be a very good reason why the market for a particular product or service seems wide open. There is perhaps good reason why the centres for fine glassware are in geologically stable Europe. Excessive heat, humidity, floods, earth-tremors are conditions that often have to be faced abroad.

Don't use your basement as a storeroom if your premises are near a river and below flood level—unless a study of records shows the flood risk to be extremely remote. An amazing number of companies run water and heating pipes over the tops of hundreds of thousands of pounds worth of furnishings, books, and materials; and they stack on the floor itself instead of on raised racks. Elementary precautions against flood damage are simple and inexpensive.

Don't avoid fire-resistant paints and materials because of their extra cost if fire is likely to be a particular hazard.

Don't, for instance, go into horticulture, with two acres of greenhouses, below an intercontinental flight path—even if speed regulations are stringent—someone might break them one day. Besides, insurance cover against sonic booms is likely to be less if you are in a danger-free area. Avoid airfield vicinities anyway—things do fall down and fuel discharge is an extra pollutant to dirty the glass. Look out for natural or man made local hazards—again, such as:

Don't have huge plate-glass frontages if your premises are between football grounds and railway stations or near pubs in rough areas, unless it's a risk that just has to be put up with.

ECONOMIC AND GOVERNMENT CHANGES

Don't rely on the fiscal policies, which encouraged your start of expansion, to keep going; and don't expect grants, loan concessions, tariff protections, etc., to go on forever. Measures introduced to speed up an economy, or to make a Government popular, can be whipped away again if the economy seems to be getting out of hand. So try to build up a buffer to increase your resistance to adverse trends by slowly establishing a lower break-even point.

Do look closely at forthcoming legislation, be aware of proposed tax or tariff changes, import restrictions. Read your trade press —it is bound to mention legislation which will affect your industry.

GEOGRAPHIC CHANGES

Do take an active interest in local affairs. That way you will know about proposals in good time. Council meetings are public and are reported in the local press. Better still, try to take part in the running of your community.

Do try to turn disadvantage to advantage. Changes mean new opportunities—if you know about them well in advance it will give you time to explore every opportunity.

Don't have too much faith in pressure groups and the power of lobbying when changes are planned. Make contingency plans just in case, and be prepared to move or adapt when the time comes. Changes have to take place, and someone has to be affected. It could be you as easily as someone else.

Don't rely on old, faithful trade. Some will stay on with you when, say, a supermarket opens in a new housing estate or regional shopping area. But you need growing, not static or dwindling business.

INDUSTRIAL ACTION IN OTHER COMPANIES

Do try to spread your customers over different industries, if you are manufacturing for industry. Manufacturing for the motor industry, or subcontracting to the ship building and repairing industry, traditionally puts a company at risk through industrial action over which it has no control at all. If you have no other baskets for your eggs, you are particularly vulnerable.

Do have contingency plans for transport upheavals.

Don't keep production going flat out when industrial action hits your chief customer—or when it begins to look inevitable. How long you keep manufacturing for stock is a fine judgement you have to make sooner or later, but an immediate slow down helps. Try to have contingency plans for your employees and for your machinery—an ancillary product for stock, taking in jobbing work, etc. Have a flexible production plan, and a flexible maintenance plan so that maintenance can be carried out in enforced idle time.

DEATH AND DOMESTIC CRISES

You really have no control at all here, and in death's case you can't even get an inkling when it is coming—other than that it is inevitable for everyone. But

Do consult your accountant and solicitor about the best ways to avoid excessive estate duty, and make sure there are similar provisions for all the shareholders. If you are working for a family firm ensure that the owners have done something about it.

Do have an atmosphere which permits understanding and sympathy between the firm and its employees at all levels. Many domestic crises can be solved by only minor considerations being shown by the company. Some firms have found tremendous advantages in such simple things as allowing foremen or shop stewards to make small loans to workshop employees, or to grant days off in times of need. This approach is equally necessary at managerial level.

Don't favour nepotism or a patriarchal set up. It might do wonders for one man's ego, but apart from discouraging everyone else, it can cause havoc when the key figure gets ill or dies. Always think of the continuation of the company, and make sure enough people know what to do should a key person suddenly not be there any longer.

Chapter 7 Reasonable Precautions Against Shared Blame

(See Part 1, Chapter 4)

The blame for the causes of decline in Chapter 4 cannot easily be put at the feet of the companies themselves, but it is equally unfair to make Fate take all the responsibility. Yet if blame is shared, and if prevention of such happenings cannot be guaranteed by any method, responsibility for at least trying, and for diminishing the effects, must fall squarely on the shoulders of managers in the companies.

BAD DEBT LOSSES

Do run a proper credit control system, and do try to get money due to you paid as early as possible, and definitely by agreed dates. It is, unfortunately, very difficult, and small companies suffer most of all. You do need those big customers, yet they are the ones that never pay early. So try to spread your customers. If possible have them in different industries.

Do try to give other incentives for large orders than long credit. And do try to reward prompt payment, and to attract new business with some other premium than an easy payment account. Collection of bad debts is expensive. Running an effective credit control system is expensive. The liquidation of a customer who owes you a lot of money can be ruinously expensive. It could be a lot cheaper to offer substantial cash discounts—or, better still, to cost on the basis of immediate payment, and add charges for different credit terms, allowing only certain customers to buy under different categories. Or perhaps you could offer free delivery to cash or thirty day customers.

Do investigate the possibility of factoring (see Chapter 15) as a solution to persistent worries about debtors.

Don't carry on supplying a customer whose debt builds up too high and who won't pay. If you feel uneasy about a customer, run a check on him through your bank. If the report is unfavourable, stop supplying immediately. Credit checks can be done easily —you don't need masses of information, but your bank will find out if his bank considers he is good for the amount of money in question. Be a bit ruthless if he is not, for it could easily also be your business that will go bust.

Don't rely too much on existing customers. Getting good new ones can be a lot cheaper than maintaining some of the bad ones.

Don't be inflexible—you might *have* to rely almost entirely on one customer or on one industry, which could land you with bad debt losses. Try to have some contingency plan, which might involve product changes, to get you going again in a new field.

Do be open with your bank manager about your difficulties with collecting debts—and it can help to confide in your major supplier too. If that is a big company, it might be able to put pressure on your debtor, or it could lead to greater understanding when you find yourself, as a result, hard pressed to pay your own debts.

LARGE-SCALE COMPETITION

Do consider carefully any approaches from large companies for selling patents, licences, or for mergers. Turning down such offers because you want to keep your independence could be signing away your company's future. If your product or service attracts such attention, it means they are serious, and are not likely to give up easily. Most companies would rather find some other way of getting in on something than through a straight fight. So if big business is interested you should get good advance warning. If that happens, but you still want to stay independent, start thinking straight away about something new, or be prepared to constantly improve your product, for a battle is inevitable.

Do try to keep one step ahead of competition with improvements. Small firms are better innovators than large companies, and are better geared for rapid and frequent changes. You won't be able to meet a big competitor in a pricing fight, so you'll have to have other advantages.

Do try to have something that only a small firm can provide. You might decide to limit your area coverage while your big competitor goes national. But in your smaller area you can perhaps offer quicker and more comprehensive service, or ancillary services to a product range.

Do consider merging in whole, or combining forces, with another small competitor. Perhaps between the two of you you can marshal enough strength or advantages to keep a large proportion of the market.

Don't get caught up in a struggle of principle. The battle of the little men might be dramatic, but the outcome is rarely as comforting as the one provided in fiction and drama. So don't sink everything in a fight to the finish. Hope to win, but be prepared to lose.

Don't give up altogether, even if you divert your main energies to some other product or service. Few firms, whatever their size ever capture more than 90 per cent of a market, for it is not only Governments that don't like monopolies. It can often pay to come back into the running after a year or more, when the big company has expanded the market and widened acceptance for the product. Besides, it is far easier to take 10 per cent of the market away from a market dominator than it is to hang on to your 50 per cent when a big company is trying to get into your field.

INDUSTRIAL ACTION IN YOUR COMPANY

Do make it a practice to be open with trade union or employees' representatives. Most industrial disputes result from poor communications, with neither side understanding or even being aware of the wants and problems of the other.

Do have frequent meetings, formal and informal, with people representing all levels in your company, and always be approachable with the minimum of procedure. Ensure there is always someone on the spot who knows exactly what sort of decisions he can take—and who is prepared to take them. Have informal meetings when other companies in similar industries are having strike trouble.

Do show yourself to be sympathetic to your employees' needs—a militant leader establishes loyalty and authority only when his fellow workers feel they are brushed aside by management.

Don't react violently when union members in your company join in a widespread strike called by their union. They probably do it with mixed feelings anyway, if industrial relations in your company have always been good.

Don't forget that small companies have natural advantages in having a high level of co-operation—use them.

Don't forget that few people work 'for a company'—just about everyone works for themselves. 'I am employed by XYZ Limited, but I work for myself'.

LOW GROSS MARGINS

Do try to have a few products with a high gross margin —difficult in the distributive trades especially, when everything operates on a small mark up, and where high turnover counts. But somewhere you need to have a reserve where, perhaps, you can counter competitive action by cutting prices on those products which have a high gross margin.

Do watch costs, gross margins, product and customer mix and management ratios very carefully. The smallest increases in overheads or in selling costs can drastically cut back profits.

Do take precautions against pilfering as well as against theft—even small losses can make a considerable difference when you are operating with low gross margins.

Don't rely too heavily on one or two customers. With low gross margins and a high turnover, a 10 per cent loss in sales could mean the loss of just about all your profit.

Don't use too few suppliers. If you are in a strongly competitive area and your supplier even marginally increases his prices, a large part of your profit margin could be absorbed if you are unable to also increase your prices—or the same could happen if you do put up your prices and you lose a few sales. On the other hand, your supplier might give you much better terms for your loyalty—but it's better to stay with him and still sell at the price you would be forced to sell at if you had to get your supplies elsewhere.

Don't try to fight bigger competitors on their terms, which are usually on prices—you don't have the margins. Try to offer some different incentive, such as a wider range of a certain type of product, or a reputation for some speciality—especially one which gives you a higher gross margin.

DECLINE IN ASSETS VALUE

Do watch out for planning and geographic changes (see Chapter 6) and forecast their implications.

Do try to adapt your premises to the needs of the area, if they are changing, and look after your assets with the same care you look after cash and stock.

Don't put unrealistic figures on assets whose value is declining —that is imaginary money, and is worthless. Take advantage of tax concessions whenever possible.

LOSS OF AGENCY OR FRANCHISE

Do make sure you know exactly why you have lost the franchise or the agency. If the franchiser is giving up the business altogether he is likely to be quite open with you, and while there might have been disadvantages in the franchise system as a whole (perhaps the difficulty of getting suitable people to take franchises) the business itself could still be sound. Or perhaps many areas were making a loss, but yours might have been much more successful. In these cases you could decide to carry on the same type of operation on your own. A record of successful trading as a franchise or agency operator would speak in your favour if you need capital to get going on your own.

But you would have to make sure the purchasing advantages, and other forms of assistance you had under the franchise were not all important. On your own your gross margins might be less, and you could be troubled by bad debts. Don't assume that a successful franchise operation would automatically become an equally successful private venture.

If you have lost the agency and it is being given to someone else in the area, or if the principal doesn't feel there is enough potential in your area, you obviously have to take a critical look at your position, and a quick decision to pull out could well be the best decision.

Do get to know other franchise holders in neighbouring areas, and take an active interest in the 'parent' company. That way you might discover if it is going badly, and would be able to prepare contingency plans.

Do try to see your operation from the franchiser's point of view. A new estate or industrial development in your area may look too good to be true, and it probably is too good to last. You might have been suitable as a franchise holder when things were quieter, but perhaps now the franchiser is being pressured into cutting up the area, by an applicant with resources and plans that far outstrip your own. An honest look at yourself and your own operation through the eyes of the licenser could forewarn you—or spur you to greater effort.

SHORTAGE OF KEY MATERIAL

Do decide whether you are going to be a manufacturer of certain products, or a specialist manufacturer working with a particular product. You can't avoid risks either way (the product could go out of fashion, or the material could run short) and in either case it would be wrong to have all your eggs in one basket. But at least it cuts down on the number of things you have to watch out for.

Do familiarise yourself with the materials used in your products. Know where they come from, what processes they undergo before they reach you. Then you can keep an eye open for any news affecting the countries of people involved in their mining, extraction, preparation, shipping, and so on.

Do keep an adequate supply, and be sure you know what reserves are kept by your nearest supplier.

Do become an avid reader of trade and technical journals, both home and overseas and of technical pages in newspapers.

Do keep a close eye on your competitors' products, and on allied products.

Do experiment with different materials from completely different sources and have contingency production and cost plans. Be versatile and flexible.

Don't take your materials for granted. You don't only have to worry about political and economic trends, but also about the extent of world resources. Know where alternative resources are, and try to obtain likely costs if these resources have to be used.

Don't rely entirely on one material. Have products made of different materials. If you specialise in a type of material, say metal castings, see what opportunities there are for you to diversify into plastic mouldings, for instance.

FRAUD

Do take a constant and searching interest in the book work of the company, however confusing or boring you might find it. Make sure you understand all financial transactions, tax, etc. Even if you couldn't do it all yourself, at least make sure you understand fully what has been done.

Do have periodic expert checks done on your books—skimping on professional accountants or auditors is often a false economy.

Do take up references and make thorough checks on people you take on who are going to be in positions of authority, and who will have financial responsibilities. And check on the givers of references too, if they are firms you haven't heard of. Do the checking yourself—a collection of impressive letters from previous employers, on their letterheads, is no guarantee.

Don't make the 'unproductive' people in your company, such as your accountant or stores manager, feel that they are less important than, say, your salesmen or production team.

Don't make your salesmen rely too heavily on getting orders to make a living. A pittance for a basic salary and everything else depending on commission causes too much anxiety, and often leads to desperation.

Don't believe in 'too good to be true' offers too readily. Few people go round offering other people fantastic bargains and chances of a lifetime. It's not a coincidence that most 'fantastic offers' require advance payments. Be sceptical.

Don't believe it can never happen to you.

MACHINERY BREAKDOWN

Do try to make some arrangement with a nearby firm (probably a bigger one) which uses similar machinery, to take up their spare capacity if you are hit by breakdowns, for it is unlikely you have much spare capacity, since you will be aiming for maximum utilisation.

Do have a contingency plan, agreed in advance with the Trade Union or employees' representative, to institute shift work if part of your plant is out of action. You could keep up production, or complete jobs on schedule if you run an extra shift in the evenings. The extra paid in overtime or bonuses is still likely to be less than the cost of lost production or a permanently dissatisfied customer.

Do be sure of replacement and repair availability from the maker.

Don't skimp on maintenance. And don't keep plant going too long. Keep a comprehensive maintenance record for each machine —sooner or later the time comes when the cost of maintenance exceeds that for a new machine on h.p. or hire.

Don't be inflexible or too independent—be prepared to hire or lease.

INSUFFICIENT CAPITAL

Do make sure that there is no way out of your predicament other than getting hold of more capital. Perhaps there is some interim improvement you can make on your product that doesn't need massive re-tooling Perhaps you can lease alternative warehouse space instead of enlarging your own—in another centre, maybe, which could give distribution advantages to offset other disadvantages. Are new vehicles essential, and do you have to buy them? What about hire or lease?

Do make sure you have explored every possible source of finance. There are many sources of capital (see Chapter 15, and our other book, *Enjoying a Profitable Business*), formal and informal—small speculative loans from friends and relatives perhaps. And there are many ways of releasing capital for other ventures, such as using hire purchase or factoring services.

Do try to estimate the long-term effects of your current lack of finance, and try to make contingency plans to tide you over if at all possible. Diverting your attention, and what capital you do have, into another direction or onto one of your other products might alter the nature of your company, but at least it might keep it alive.

Do be sure you know exactly what your needs are—your immediate capital need might only be stage one, and there could be more capital needs later. Gearing up to meet competition, for instance, could put you in a race whose pace you'll never be able to sustain, even if you get in the running for a year or two. Your immediate capital shortage might be a blessing in disguise and could provide you with the impetus to change direction, sell some assets, and start in a new field.

Don't assume you must meet competition on its own ground. Less money, better spent, perhaps on another salesman or two, or on a carefully worked out product promotion system, might be an adequate substitution.

Don't be complacent about your position, and don't believe that the status quo will do 'for another year'. Plant modernisation when you can afford it might make profits look slim, but you could be thankful in a lean year that you took that step.

GROWTH IN SIZE

Do try to plan ahead, and know why your plans are what they are. And do be sure they are what you really want them to be. Try to be realistic and knowledgeable about the implications of your ambitions. You need to do a lot of self questioning —regularly ask yourself questions such as 'How did the firm get to where it is now; what is its exact status in industry and in the immediate environment; where are we going; how will we get there; what are our long-term objectives?'

Do be sure what your main objective is—to grow and grow, or to provide a 'hobby', to provide employment for yourself and others, or to prove your abilities and fulfil your aspirations.

Do make known to your senior managers your long-term objectives, and how you think they might be reached—and listen to their comments. It is so easy to have some objective in your mind for so long, and to have such burning ambition, that you can be completely blind to obvious implications.

Do communicate with your employees. Much of the loss of atmosphere and loyalty is due to poor communications, and bigger pay packets and promotion don't always compensate for an impression of being left out of things. In most small companies, all employees feel very much a part of the company, so let people know in good time about any changes that might be coming up, and why you are making the changes. This is never so necessary as when you introduce intermediate levels of authority—a step that becomes inevitable with significant expansion.

Do try to make the changes gradual and acceptable. If your men on the shop floor have been used to settling problems directly with the production director, who has always spent three or four hours a day in the workshop, don't suddenly introduce a workshop manager in between—it's unfair on him as well as on his men. Let them all work together for a while. Don't suddenly shut doors that have always been open before.

Don't unblinkingly believe that the only pursuit and aim of business is constant growth. There are thousands of firms which have developed an individuality and have steadily but not dramatically increased their turnover, and have perhaps only slowly increased their profits. But they have hardly failed —they have established an unshakeable clientele which is constantly being replenished they provide enviable working conditions and are repaid by equally enviable loyalty, they have the respect and affection of their community. All this —and more—could easily have been thrown away if they had gone all out for growth.

Don't make changes too late. Don't carry on as a small firm when you have almost reached the stage of being a medium-sized firm—and want to become one. If you do, it means everyone is working extra hard and yet when you inevitably have to make changes, new personnel are going to be introduced, the rapid salary increases the original staff were compensated with for their extra efforts are going to slow down or stop, and everyone will be caught up in a flurry of procedural changes and new documentation. Disenchantment will rapidly follow bewilderment.

Don't forget that more customers usually means more money owed to you; and that more sales means more purchases.

Don't expect small firm flexibility and informality with big firm turnover and status.

Don't take on more than you are absolutely certain you can handle —whether orders or responsibilities.

Don't forget the rapid escalation of overheads when you contemplate such rosy attractions as doubling customers, turnover or output.

Don't isolate one aspect of the firm from the others—a vast increase in sales will also mean an increase in warehousing, transport, production, storage, administration. Special purchasing arrangements might no longer be possible if your habitual supplier of a particular material or product can't meet your new requirements. Staff for one of your activities might be difficult to get, and so hold up other activities.

TWILIGHT YEARS

Do try to always have someone considerably younger than the rest in the top management team—or close to it. A personal assistant—perhaps a graduate trainee—is often a good way of being kept on your toes. It doesn't matter if the person doesn't have a string of qualifications, or experience. The danger is that enthusiasm will be lost, and if you take on someone whose enthusiasm far outweighs his experience, he will still be contributing a great deal. He is also less likely to accept 'because it's always been done that way' as a valid reason for doing anything.

Do be on the lookout for signs of boredom and apathy—in yourself as well as others. Lackadaisical air blows gently, but travels far.

Don't resist change—it's going on all the time, all around you. Customers change, needs and wants change, materials and production techniques change. Sources of supply change. Markets and products change. Opportunities change. What was impossible yesterday could well be possible today, or tomorrow.

Don't be too proud or slow to hand over the reins. There is more skill needed to judge, choose and train new managers than there is to simply keep on carrying out old familiar routines.

Don't be over-sentimental towards colleagues—or yourself. You have a duty towards any shareholders and to all your employees. Perhaps a part-time retainer, or an occasional advisory position would soften the blow of having to give over to a younger team. And there is always the excitement of starting up a new, small venture. . . .

Chapter 8 Preventing Your Own Errors

(See Part 1, Chapter 5)

Although none of us likes to admit making mistakes or wrong judgements, there are some things that go wrong which simply cannot honestly be blamed on anyone or anything else —the Causes of failure in Chapter 5 for instance. And many people would blame even more on poor management than is covered in that chapter. The easiest way to avoid blaming yourself is take precautions and prevent any of the causes from taking effect. Easier said than done, but. . . .

HIGH AND CHANGING BREAK-EVEN

Do keep a frequent check on all costs. Cost control is vital, but you can't even have that without cost knowledge. It means lots of documents to be filled in, perhaps, but it is worth it.

Do try constantly to achieve a *lower* break-even point—that way you might at least manage to keep the present point constant.

Do relate the estimated break-even point with realistic conditions. There is no point in, say, launching a new product with a high break-even point simply because there is no immediate competition and you want to establish your product with low price. If the product or service is any good at all, there soon will be competition. Then with your sales also going up and your overheads increasing through extra trading, and through increased expenditure trying to outsell competition, you will be faced with an even higher break-even point—at the very moment you wish you could cut prices to take the wind out of your competitor's sails.

Don't forget that the older a product gets, the less easy it is to keep it profitable with a high break-even point. Orders lost to competition, or simple market saturation speed the end of the sales graphs' upward sweep. That is the time when you want something in reserve, so always be on the lookout for ways to reduce the unit cost—even when you feel you are operating comfortably within budgeted margins.

Don't be caught without plans up your sleeve for any sudden rises in different costs—materials, labour, transport. The higher your break-even point, the less latitude you have for taking in such increases.

MARKET DOMINATION

Do appreciate the pitfalls ahead of you when you are a market leader. You will be constantly under attack, and need as much as anyone else to have a reserve in your gross margin.

Do remember that if you have the lion's share of a market, it is easier for a new competitor to take away 5 or 10 per cent of your sales than it is for you to increase your sales by a similar amount. You will have to rely almost entirely on getting your equivalent share of the expanding market to keep growing, and need that share and constant cost cutting to increase your profitability—even to maintain it.

Do keep looking out for new products and diversification. When a market stops expanding, the market leader is the first to feel the calm, and practically nothing it can do will prevent sales from dropping from that moment. So you should be ready to immediately divert energies to building up another source of revenue. Even better, you should, from experience and from knowledge of your markets, have an accurate measure of the lead time in product and market development, and an estimate of the product life cycle. You could then plan your new product to establish itself shortly before the old product's expansion begins to slow down.

Don't be complacent about being a market leader. Even if yours is one of those rare companies which leads the field by such a degree that it seems unassailable, you still have to watch competition for product or service innovation. If you have a virtual monopoly on sales, that doesn't mean you necessarily have a monopoly on good ideas.

Don't go all out for domination with only one service or product. There is usually more satisfaction, peace of mind, profits, and the enjoyment of flexibility in being a strong competitor to a number of different leaders than there is in being one leader.

Don't forget that if you are a successful market leader, there will always be a number of people casting covetous looks at your position, and that, for your customers, a chance to try something different or to identify with a challenger often has more appeal than brand loyalty.

TOO LITTLE DIVERSIFICATION

Do look again at the lines on 'Causes' and 'Prevention' for such things as 'Large-scale competition,' 'Loss of agency of franchise,' 'Shortage of key materials,' 'High and changing break-even', 'Market domination.'

Do have plans for re-directing your activities, even if you are a successful one-product company. Not everyone can play safe to such a degree that, come what may, they can always fall back on something else (besides, training, personal abilities, knowledge, available resources, and many other things dictate that there must be some degree of specialisation); and diversification does not necessarily mean going to the degree of having half your company relying on products for the motor trade, while the other half relies on feeding tourists. Diversification can mean being in more than one area, having more than one or two big customers, being in different branches of the same business (such as catering to DIY enthusiasts as well as to the building trade), or having different types of distribution. A proper product mix is an essential ingredient of any successful company.

Don't put all your eggs in one basket.

CHANGING MARKETS AND MATERIALS

Do keep up to date with the trade and technical literature in your field. It is very rare indeed for no-one at all to publish some indication of forthcoming changes.

Do really know your whole market—this is very much different from knowing your customers. Even that is hard enough, for they can change likes and dislikes. You also have to know who doesn't buy your products, and why. You have to know what markets are like in other countries and decide whether trends are going to be repeated in your market place—and if so, when.

Do watch carefully the activities of all your competitors. Far and near, and fringe competitors as well. The toy car industry in Britain was really caught out with the American improvements with freer running toy cars. It is impossiblle to believe they didn't know such things existed, and they soon showed (just in time) they too could make them.

Do carefully follow all developments in the refinement of new materials. A material you write off this year could have advanced considerably by next year. What cannot be done easily or economically with a new material—or even an old one—could be made possible with just one development made by an entirely different industry. Just look back over even five years at the way familiar, everyday things have changed in appearance, shape, materials. 'Plastic' once was a derogatory term—now a dozen different materials are loosely called plastic, yet bear little resemblance to the old, brittle, weak stuff, and many are infinitely more versatile and better suited than the traditional materials which they have rapidly replaced. New alloys are constantly appearing, new processes make them cheaper, more adaptable.

Do take frequent critical and sceptical looks at your own products or services. Do listen to criticism, and encourage customer comments. Praise might warm your heart, but complaints can be far more rewarding in the long run.

Don't resist change, or believe in 'the old order' never changing. The greatest developments in turnover and the growth of new companies comes not so much from new management techniques, bigger populations or more effective selling, but from technological development and changing markets—markets that have changed because new groups have become new consumers, and because technological developments have put more products and services within the range of more people's pockets. If new opportunities have come your way because of this, present complacency could leave you behind while progress flows on.

Don't forget that other firms using different materials are always on the lookout for new products to make with these materials—yours might be one of them, and suddenly you'll find yourself with a new, powerful and energetic competitor.

INVESTMENT IN SPECIALIST PLANT

Do see this as another of the hazards inherent in too little diversification. It is bad enough to lose a major portion of your sales if the bottom falls out of your market. Having most of your plant capable only of one or two specialised uses means you will lose a large slice of your assets as well.

Do look into the possibilities of subcontracting part of your manufacturing, packaging, or whatever calls for specialist equipment. It might not work out that much more costly, and could perhaps allow you to use more versatile plant for the remainder of the process, or for diversification.

Do explore every possibility within the scope of your equipment, so that if you do have to use specialist plant, you can turn that into an asset. Its capabilities might lead you to new products in a different market, or you might in turn be able to do jobs for other companies.

Don't rely too much on your specialised product and the unusual plant it needs being a defence against competitors entering your field. If there is a demand for your product or service, firms that hesitate to invest in such equipment are likely to concentrate on looking for alternative methods. If they find them you could be left with idle and almost worthless plant.

Don't automatically replace any of your specialised equipment without first convincing yourself that there is really no other way of doing the job. Developments in other equipment or in materials could have opened up new solutions.

MARKET SATURATION

Do keep a close eye on the whole market, on the number of competitors and on their performance. You have to know, as accurately as possible, what your share of the market is, before any estimate of the size of the market can be made. And a slow down in your own sales doesn't necessarily mean the end of the line. Just as an unexpected jump in sales could be something to worry about rather than to rejoice over, for it could be caused by the departure of a wary competitor who has kept his ear close to the ground.

Do know well the lead times for new product development and production, so that you are sure to have a new development ready for the market to replace a 'tired' product.

Don't try to squeeze the very last sales from an existing but obviously declining market. Accurate control documentation will enable you to draw your own product life cycle (see Fig. 3).
Your new product should be timed to start its growth at the time when your existing product has reached maturity. A good knowledge of the market could allow you to 're-launch'

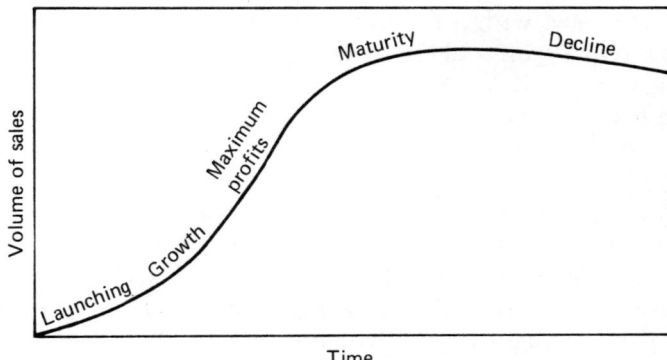

Figure 3. A typical product life cycle

your existing product, if a brand-new product is going to be difficult or expensive to launch, or if your timing has been a bit wrong, or if the current state of the market leads you to think it is not the right time to bring out a new product. Your product life cycle would then look something like Fig. 4. Whatever your tactics, don't try to press on while the curve gets into the horizontal stage without having some new marketing venture. Cost cutting at that stage is not going to achieve much.

(Your knowledge of your market will give you a reasonable

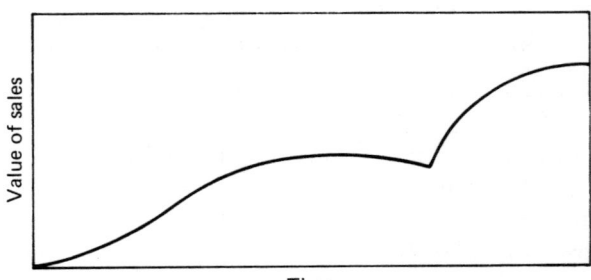

Figure 4. Product life cycle with effect of innovation and renewed marketing activity

estimate of the time span of the life cycle, since it varies greatly from one industry to another. The market life cycle for various garden tools could stretch 10 years or more, only minor alterations being necessary since there is little that can be done with a spade, for instance, that might make a buyer think it is newer and better than the next one. Publishers, on the other hand, are faced with a life cycle on a new title of perhaps as little as two months between launch and the fall in rate of buying. As much as there can be an average, five years is probably a reasonable span for a product life cycle.)

Don't keep on relying on your original projections for a market size and life, made before you began activity in the market. Market projections need to be constantly revised and updated, and depend so much on competitive action, and on the changing nature of the market. It can also be significantly affected by changes on the fringe of the market. The health and fitness market undergoes constant revival, perhaps as new batches of people approach middle age, perhaps because will power comes in collective waves. But each revival, short though it might be, still manages to accommodate three or four fads. The market for each one is initially huge, and spectacular growth follows launching almost immediately—until someone comes up with some entirely different gadget which claims the attention of all those who were still about to buy the first one.

Don't forget to watch out for product saturation as well as market saturation—they are not always the same.

RELIANCE ON TOO FEW CUSTOMERS

Do examine your selling costs, the discounts you give. Your customer mix is as important as your product mix. The difficulty you are having in maintaining your budgeted gross margin might be due to the high discounts you are giving on the large proportion of your sales. The source of all your trouble might be the one firm you silently bless each time you do a sales forecast—your number one customer.

Do try to get a spread of customers in different industries, so that you won't automatically be hit hard if one industry goes through a hard time.

Do take this opportunity to instigate a carefully thought out discount system. If you are going after new customers, start off the way you wish to carry on.

Do also take the opportunity to get in money owed you—and lay down rigid rules about credit. It is always difficult to be unbending with one or two customers who give you most of your business, and yet if they fall behind in their payments, you are likely to be in great difficulties.

Don't get used to the steady re-orders of a large customer. The success of your business then depends on the success of his business—you've really lost your independence. And you develop an unreal operation, with costs geared to a set of conditions very much different from what they would be if your customer mix were more varied.

Don't base your costs and method of operation on your experience with one big customer when you are planning to spread your net. You are likely to need more salesmen. Delivery and packaging costs are likely to increase at a different proportion to any increases in sales that might result. Administration will cost more. But you can save on discounts and on credit facilities.

Don't lose sight of the whole market through too long and close contact with one customer. It is all too easy to make changes in your product to suit him, but they might be worthless, or even detract from your product's appeal when you go to other customers.

Don't put all your eggs in one basket.

USING TOO FEW SUPPLIERS

Do have alternative sources of supply for everything you need. As with choosing customers, so you should not lose your independence by relying so greatly on one other firm. It is especially sad to find yourself dependent on your supplier.

Do get regular quotations from other sources, and look at their products. Loyalty to a brand—whether it is a component of your products, a line that you resell, office equipment or a window cleaning service—is comforting to those you consistently give your money to. But your prime responsibility is to your firm, your shareholders, your employees.

Do see salesmen as a matter of course—fix a rota and make it known, insist on brief factual presentations. But do see them. You never know what you are missing.

Don't readily base your unit cost calculations and your break-even point on prices you know you are only getting because you are an old and faithful buyer from a particular company. It's a nice situation to be in and you shouldn't look a gift horse in the mouth, but it is making you dependent on the continued success of your supplier. He might go out of business, he might suddenly have to cut down on his generous discount terms, he might be taken over. You will be faced with a sudden rise in costs that haven't affected anyone else in your market.

Don't accept your supplier's recommendations for changes to your product that will fit in with his own plans without carefully studying the implications. Component manufacturers can often make very good cost reduction suggestions, but be careful that the tail doesn't wag the dog.

LACK OF EXPANSION PLANS

Do transfer some of your grandest optimism and extravagant daydreams to paper. There is no point in being optimistic and aiming for expansion if you don't know what to do when it comes.

Do consider all aspects of expansion, not only what you will do with the increased turnover. For every sales projection you should have a costs projection.

Do work out the realistic limitations of each department. Get each department head to budget for the estimated year ahead, but also for estimated plus 10 and perhaps even 20 per cent. And add a bit yourself to each cost and subtract a bit for each person's output. There are always unforeseen things that crop up, administration always seems to increase out of all proportion, and people hardly ever work quite as hard as they intended to or wish they would.

Do make sure that all the resources needed will actually be available. Even if you know you can take care of rises in costs, you need to be sure that you can get the extra personnel, the extra warehousing, the extra factory floor space, the extra distribution facilities.

Don't work out present gross margins and break-evens on conditions which you know will not apply if hoped for growth does come. Everything can be lost by finding you have to increase your selling prices just as you are starting to get established.

Don't expand beyond your confidently known capabilities. Expansion followed by consolidation followed by expansion might not be as dramatically exciting as expanding in leaps and bounds, but it makes a lot more business sense.

INSUFFICIENT CONTROLS, AND FIGURE BLINDNESS

Do insist on detailed budgets from every department.

Do make sure you know what the whole market is doing, what your competitors' growth figures are. It is all to easy to gain comfort from your own increasing turnover—until you find that while you have been growing at 5 per cent a year, everyone else has been growing at 10 per cent.

Do keep accurate, comprehensive and up-to-date control documents—or have someone else keep them for you, but study them regularly. Study your bank balance sheet regularly, and choose five or six management ratios that reflect the relation of various costs to sales, and work them out regularly.

Don't hoodwink yourself into believing downward trends are seasonal fluctuations and upward trends are solid signs of growth. It is a human failing to do so, but unfortunately the reverse is often the real truth.

NOT SEEING THE WHOLE MARKET

Do read extensively in the trade press. Go to meetings of your Association or Society, and of your Chamber of Commerce. A lot of business can be done in the bar or on the golf course, especially by picking up hints which influence your own decisions.

Do try to always look at your market through the eyes of someone who is thinking of starting up in it. Seeing it only through your own eyes gives a distorted picture, and you might easily get the wrong idea of its growth rate and its potential. Look at the number of new competitors, and your own increase in sales to get an idea of your own position.

Don't be satisfied with your growth rate unless you know what the growth rate for the whole market is. You don't necessarily have to grow as fast as the whole market—that might not be your policy, you might have a definite plan to limit your own growth rate. But your growth rate is usually meaningless unless you can relate it to the whole market. Growing at 20 per cent while the market grows at 25 per cent might be your policy—but you might find one day that the market growth has slipped to 10 per cent and you are plunging ahead into a saturated market that your competitors have abandoned.

WRONG DECISIONS IN BAD TIMES

A bit unfair perhaps to put it down to your fault—the way things go you could just as well have been right. But inevitably people will say 'Oh, he made the wrong decision, and . . .' So,

Do try to be well informed as to what is going on in the broadest sense. This doesn't mean that you have to develop an expertise in fundamentals of macro economics and international finance, since even the experts don't agree that all of them understand it. But you must know what sparks off slumps, whether they are local, national or international, and what the consensus of opinion is about the duration and trends of the slump. Perhaps this seems to be stating the obvious, for everyone keeps up-to-date on current affairs—or do they? With pressures at work, a few late evenings at work, a couple of meetings, social life, the snatches of news you pick up for five or six days might be about international strife and little else. Suddenly a crisis is a *fait accompli*, and you have to make decisions based on sketchy background information.

Do try to keep an open mind and weigh up the arguments and opinions of the most experienced experts when making your decisions. We all like to form our own opinions and solutions on social, political and international affairs—and often the outcome really is anyone's guess—but just as we would consult others, or read extensively, when up against a manufacturing problem we are not experienced with, so wider consultation through listening and reading is essential during social or economic trends which affect different branches of industry. For most of the year, it is difficult to find the time, the inclination or the money to read a broad selection of papers, and weeklies such as *The Economist, New Society, New Statesman* and *Spectator*, as well as the trade and technical papers. But the extra effort, especially with the first one, perhaps, is worth it. And read 'the other sides'' papers and weeklies too, however much they annoy you. Decisions are based on facts, and the more you have the better. All sorts of influences work towards the solution of problems that affect a large segment of the population, and knowledge about those influences, as well as about the problem itself, is vital. You don't have to follow some expert's way of thinking, but acceptance or rejection of advice or predictions is itself a decision which has to be carefully taken. And, of course, these are not infallible—there are so many differences of opinion that some have to be wrong. The decisions you make will be your decisions, and you won't be able to blame anyone else for them —but the more information they can be based on, the easier it will be to make them.

Do explain the problem you are faced with as fully as possible to the people that will be affected. Obviously it will be discussed over and over again at management meetings, but involve the representatives of all your employees as well. If they have been brought into the picture right from the start, and understand the difficulties, it could soften later attitudes.

Don't 'wait and see' for too long without doing anything. Precipitate action is frequently foolhardy, but so is carrying on as if nothing was wrong. Have phased plans drawn up and implement them early. Manufacturing at normal production rates for stock is sure to lead to later crises, for you'll have to sell your normal levels plus all the extra. An early cut back means less likelihood of having to make anyone redundant later.

Don't be too ready to change your mind. A carefully thought out decision, with a proper plan of action has many virtues and changing decisions from day to day or week to week is almost as bad as not making any decision at all. At least never alter a decision until the new set of implications has been equally carefully thought about.

EXCESSIVE CREDIT AND BAD DEBTS

Do have a specific credit policy which your customers and potential customers know well. It can be flexible, but with reason, and because of defined circumstances.

Do spend time and effort on setting up a credit control system. With decimalisation, there are many very simple and inexpensive accounting machines which can do debtors' analysis with ease. At the moment, you should be able to know exactly how much you are owed, and be able to extract overdue accounts for consideration. Sales, too, should get in the habit of being aware of credit control problems.

Do have a proven system of satisfying yourself about a customer's credit-worthiness. Some firms blithely open accounts for jobs costing as little as £5. Others won't open an account for initial purchases of less than £20—but then they do not run a proper check on the new customer's finances and get taken for £25 instead. Your bank manager can be invaluable here—he can't get detailed account information from your customer's bank, but all you need is the normal extent of your customer's monthly purchases to find out whether he is likely to be able to pay. Consistent non-payers, even when they can afford it, also get known, and a check on references and through your bank should easily disclose this.

Don't be too keen to rush into sales and so into an impossible credit situation. Easy credit and repayment terms should never be a selling point, unless you have budgeted for a realistic loss by bad debts, for a loss of interest money, and have enough capital to take care of your own debts. And be wary of the customer who insists on long credit terms as a condition of purchase. Is he genuinely trying to make maximum use of working capital, or is he in such a situation that he's hoping for "Something to turn up" before he has to pay?

LACK OF PROPER INSURANCE COVER

Do realise that this is the only control you have over the effect of natural disasters, catastrophes and inevitable acts of Nature.

Do take into account loss of profits as well as of property when taking out insurance. Also remember coverage for lost accounts, goodwill, the cost of new premises or equipment, possible redundancies and so on, when you discuss insurance with your agent.

Don't put too much faith in luck and chance. It is luck and chance that send catastrophe your way.

ADVERSE PERSONAL FACTORS

Do recognise human, and therefore your, shortcomings. Be critical and sometimes introspective. Honesty with your own failings is as important as appreciating and making fullest use of your talents and abilities.

Do make up for your own shortcomings by a careful selection of senior personnel. Working with someone who is just like you might be more enjoyable and easy on your mind, but it doesn't do the company much good.

Don't be slow to delegate those things that you know you are weakest in. Proper staff selection, and an ability and readiness to delegate are among the most important management attributes.

Part 3 THE CURE—NINE ROUTES TO A QUICK RECOVERY

If this book has played its part properly up to here, you should now be in a position to start building up your company's strength again. With the cause of decline identified and, hopefully, done away with (never to return?) your energies can be turned to making a quick recovery. At this stage the emphasis can be very much on the speed of recovery, so the following chapters deal mainly with ways and means of getting things moving again, of restoring confidence in the company. For confidence plays a big part—if you, your employees, your banker, your creditors and your investors have confidence in the company, it will be a lot easier to get customers to have confidence too—and from confidence comes sales.

Later on, in Chapter 18 and 19, there are some hints about progressively building up a company's strength over a long period, but this is basically the subject matter of our first book, *Enjoying a Profitable Business*. These following chapters do not pretend to give the solution to better business—to some extent the answer to your problems (if there is one) is likely to be the opposite of their causes. Identifying the causes of slack or declining business as poor morale, lack of capital for expansion and a burden of bad debts implies the solution is to get in your debts, use that money plus some borrowed to expand the business, so boosting morale as well as sales. If only it was so simple.

Chapter 9 Bridging Plans

It often seems as if most working time is taken up dealing with endless day to day affairs, but business cannot be run on a day to day basis. Admittedly, bridges can't be crossed until you get to them, but the person who knows what bridges he's likely to encounter and is prepared for them is going to get further faster than any haphazard traveller. Before you make any drastic reorganisation, invest substantial amounts of time and money, or get involved in five year plans, you should be clear about your motives and objectives. This is a good moment to ask yourself:

Do I want to stay with/keep this company?
Does it suit me?
Do I want to stay in this type of activity?
What are my liabilities?
What are my personal advantages and disadvantages?
What am I good at—selling, making, developing?
What are my assets—in men, money and machines?
Are my assets compatible with my operations and objectives?
   (If they're not, don't automatically assume it is best to change your objectives—that could be an easy step to years of dissatisfaction and consequently mediocre performance.)

How much time can I allow myself to get where I want to be?

These are largely personal questions—to have analysed the faults in your firm, you will already have asked some pretty searching questions about the market, your products, your competitors, the firm itself. At this point, things that are important are determination, motivation, objectives, clarity of purpose. (Anyone who has done some DIY job around the house, or built models, knows how much smoother everything seems to go if you sit down with tools, materials and plans for a while until you are absolutely sure what you are going to do —and that you really do want to do it.)

NEED FOR SHORT-TERM PLANS

Whatever your answers add up to, you will need to make short-term plans to get into a strong position from which to carry out your long-term strategy. If you want things to be as they are, only better, you'll need to inject a new zest into the company and its people by showing a rapid improvement in income/expenditure ratios, and by clearing the decks for new products, new markets, new techniques. If you decide the company as a whole needs a radical change, your changeover plans are going to be as important to the company's future as the long-range plans will be, once it's got going again in its new activity. Any changeover will have to be financed quite heavily—perhaps by new equipment, but certainly by entering a new market. For a company that has perhaps not been too healthy, the finance for such a try for new life may not easily come from traditional sources, and the decision may have to be made to take short-term measures to dramatically improve profitability—measures that would be foolish on a long-term basis or if you were going to stay in the same activity indefinitely, but which would give you the necessary immediate finance or create conditions which would encourage others to finance you. And if your decision is that the only thing to do is to sell up and start all over again with something completely different, then you will need to do a dressing-up operation to be able to show attractive turnover and profit figures. But if you are thinking of attracting a merger offer, rather than an outright buyer, you will be less anxious about profits and put more attention on making the company attractive as a stable long-term investment.

CONTROLLING PROGRESS

There are two equally important parts in any planning exercise. One is naturally the plan itself, and the other is the system for controlling progress. There is little use in carefully mapping out a route for a touring holiday and then leaving the map behind or never following your progress on it. So with your bridging plans. Later on, if you don't have them already, you will have to set up some efficient system of control documentation to monitor your long- and short-term plans. But the bridging plans are important too. Different objectives focus attention on different activities, and you want to be sure you are getting the right information from which to act on day to day decisions, and to know how close you are getting to your objective.

So now you have a rough idea of what your aim is, have decided on the interim measure to get you to the right stage from which you can best set out for your ultimate objective, and are thinking of how you will best monitor progress through this bridging stage, which might be one of quickly increasing profits, preparing for heavy investment, getting ready for a drastic product changeover, looking for buyers or would-be mergers. Whatever the objectives of this stage are, they will almost certainly require a quick and noticeable improvement in some aspect of the company's activities (after all, if there were no faults, there would be no need of such bridging plans). The next chapters give some hints on how this can be achieved.

Chapter 10 Cost Cutting

A higher gross margin makes business life a lot easier. That comfortable gap between the total cost of your product or service and the price you sell it for, means a lower break-even point and, if sales carry on well beyond the break-even stage, a healthy profit which can provide for expansion and knock down debts and overdraft.

These three elements—costs, income and the difference between the two—govern practically every business action, but often two of them get forgotten in a flat-out pursuit of the remaining one. This can negate the object of the exercise (presumably to increase profits), because it is the balance between all three that is important.

Engineering a higher gross margin by cutting costs is often the only way open in a competitive situation, and it also has the advantage of showing quicker results than can be got by increasing the selling price (which can usually only be done with new stocks). Consequently (and because costs always have a habit of creeping up and reducing gross margins even during periods of normal, healthy business) there can hardly be a company which is not periodically shaken by a cost reduction drive.

COST CUTTING DANGERS

A high proportion of cost reduction drives are seven-day wonders which are ultimately ineffective—or worse. A directorial memo thunders through the company after a bad set of trading figures and endless petty regulations come into power. Stationery is put under guard, expenses are scrutinised and salesmen move into class C hotels. A cheaper type of paint is used for the annual face lift and engineers spend another day on designs trying to get more patterns out of standard sheets of metal. Purchases are held over and creditors' patience is stretched to breaking point.

At the end of that month a delighted management sees a significant drop in expenditure and takes this new figure as the new norm which brings a rush of confidence. At about the same time all sorts of people are finding that the dozens of restrictions are becoming a burden and even causing other, more important work to pile up. Stationery becomes freely available again and draughtsmen are busy with greater things. Accounts are paid more quickly because the accounts department is tired of being the butt of creditors' wrath. Sale force morale slips and one or two leave for competitors whose salesmen seem to be having a far better life in the field. Within a couple of months costs have gone up again—even higher than the last high which started all the panic.

Other companies who might pride themselves on seeing costs on a much grander scale can get into equally deep waters. Office mechanisation is often the hidden reef that they founder on. With promises—or at least strong indications —that they will cut the cost of running their accounts department by 30 per cent if they mechanise, or use a computer bureau, the whole firm is turned upside down for six months while every document and administrative procedure is changed over for the sake of expected salvation. A year and countless headaches later the gross margin has barely budged.

These two types of cost reduction efforts can easily fail —because what is being attacked is a minor cost centre, and not a major one. (Of course, in some types of business, administration can be a major cost, but even here not much is going to be achieved by, say, cutting back on the consumption of paper clips.) Cost consciousness always seems to centre around items that are not recognisably connected with revenue, or which don't seem in any way to be 'productive'. Much maligned administration is perennially first on the list —administration never shows a 'profit' therefore it is an expense, therefore to reduce expenses cut the cost of administration. But with 10 per cent of revenue being an average budget for administration there's not much that can be done there that will make a noticeable dent in overall expenses. And put next to salaries, rents and maintenance the saving of a few reams of paper and a dozen typewriter ribbons isn't going to have much impression on that 10 per cent either.

The other danger with this sort of 'first thought of, first cut' cost reduction exercise is that its effect is short term—too short a term, even for the purpose of these chapters where we are looking for some way of getting a timely upturn in fortunes. A company that is trying to establish confidence (its own and others' in itself) is not going to get far by being overdue with paying its debts, by sending out faintly typed letters on poor quality paper and by having disgruntled salesmen in shabby cars.

THE POTENTIAL IN COST CUTTING

The right way is the opposite of the wrong way. Just as you can't put right a fault until you have identified the fault and found its cause, you can't effectively cut costs until you have identified the major cost areas, and their costs breakdown. This will be impossible without good documentation, which will also be required if you are trying to counter a trend of rising costs. It's not enough to know that production accounts for the greatest single expenditure—you need a complete breakdown of production costs before you can start trying to trim.

A cost cutting programme needs careful planning, and should be carried out with a surgeon's sensitivity rather than with a lumberjack's brute force. It requires careful planning, tact, and patient perseverance. Some measures are bound to be drastic and they should be temporary, but since the whole exercise is an attempt to get costs down to a level—giving a satisfactory return on investment, you should persevere with the vigilance you use during the campaign, and constantly review costs. Within sensible limits though—moderation in all things. Looking around some companies, you can often anticipate the managing director's boast 'We're a very cost conscious bunch here, you know'. Like their purses, their faces are pinched, and it is doubtful whether any 'cost conscious' company has ever been as successful (with all that entails) as 'growth conscious' companies.

DO'S AND DON'TS

Analyse all costs to get positive identification of the major expenses, and try to get a similar breakdown for the last three or five years. Keep a detailed analysis of all costs so that you can notice and act against any rising trend.

Don't have blanket and undefined cost reduction campaigns. Identify certain costs and attempt to cut those costs. 'We've got to cut costs and we shall cut costs' should only be a warm up statement, but often it turns out to be the whole directive.

Plan exactly how you are going to reduce the costs you have singled out, by listing everything you can think of which will have that effect. Don't simply resolve to 'spend less'. Appoint a 'good housekeeping' committee to investigate possible schemes.

Make sure you know what the implications will be of whatever you do to cut costs. You don't want to cut one cost only to find another growing in its place, or to find that you will miss delivery dates or schedules.

Have a definite target amount by which you plan to cut costs, and fix a reasonable time limit for the campaign.
Even though only one sector accounts for substantial costs, it is worthwhile to identify major proportionate costs in each department in your company and have campaigns to cut them too. This will increase the level of cost awareness throughout the firm, and will stop any group feeling they have been sin-

gled out for 'restrictions'.

Offer incentives for successful cost cutting—bonuses for departments that reach (and stay on) their cut level, perhaps. Or offer cash prizes to anyone offering suggestions which successfully cut costs in the company by a certain percentage.

There is no harm in having drives against petty costs, for they can escalate to anything but petty proportions. But keep such campaigns in perspective. Don't give them 'major directive' status and certainly don't put them on the same level as the planned, specific cost cutting exercises.

Try to distinguish between cutting costs and postponements in expenditure. Temporary shortages of cash, or immediate needs to reflect higher profits can be met by holding off many various expenses. But these shouldn't be given the status of cost reductions. If at all possible, items singled out for cost cutting should be those that can 'stay cut'. Knowing that some measures can only be temporary is bound to reduce long term attention to everything else associated with it.

Think carefully about morale in any cost reduction campaigns. Not everyone sees virtue in hardship or is spurred on by a Spartan existence. Don't be penny wise and pound foolish.

Emphasise the positive side of cost reduction—reducing costs increases gross margins, and *increases* profits.

Don't forget that the real object is not simply to reduce expenditure, but to reduce the expenditure/sales ratio. If any action you take to cut costs will also cut turnover, at least make sure the proportions are favourable.

The most effective steps to take might not be those which show early results. Potential investors and others you wish to impress can be just as enthusiastic over definite signs, even further investment, which point to some future dramatic reduction in costs. But be sure you are aware of all costs, especially those almost unrelated ones, if you go for, say, automated systems. Don't forget the disruption costs, training costs, possible compensations to employees, new expansion costs, replacement costs, adaptations to premises, mainten-ance, insurance, and so on.

Sales

Biggest expenses likely to be salesmen.
What is their break-even point?
What is their cost expressed as percentage of sales?
Is their training good enough?
Have their routes been properly planned?
Are your customers graded so that some are called on once a month—twice a month?
Are their territories being effectively covered, or is there too much to-ing and fro-ing?
Are you trying to cover too large an area?
Would you lose anything by cutting down the area or number of calls each salesman is expected to cover by altering the call frequency on different types of account?
Are all your customers worth keeping?
How many new accounts do you open per month?
Are you giving too high discounts?
Are you losing some gross margin by delivering too many small orders to distant customers?
Are you pricing according to size of accounts, frequency and size of order?
Are you keeping separate small turnover products going for the sake of only a few customers?
Is your advertising going to too many people who are never likely to be customers?
What is its cost expressed as a percentage of sales?
Have you any means (reply coupons, etc.) of measuring the effectiveness of your advertising?

Production

Have you explored all possibilities for batch production?
Are you producing too many lines or variations?
Have you tried to rationalise designs to give better batch pro-duction runs?
Are there any false economies going on, with machines having

too much idle time through maintenance and repair, slowness through blunt cutting tools?

Are working conditions conducive to high steady output?

Could the factory floor layout be improved to give a smoother work flow?

Could you manufacture your various products for stock in rotation to give longer runs and save machine change-over time?

Could idle time on certain machines be used on outside jobbing work or regular sub-contracting, even on completely different products?

Would quality control at intermediate stages cut down on wasted work?

Are materials being wasted through careless design?

When materials are cut in the most efficient way, is there anything else that can be done with the off-cuts?

Have all products you manufacture been designed with overall rationalisation of materials in mind?

Have you recently reviewed the cost and effectiveness of all alternative types of materials?

Can you utilise your unavoidable scrap in any way – resale, re-use, packaging?

Are your maintenance schedules planned to cause the minimum disruption to production schedules?

Do you carry out effective preventative maintenance?

Do designers and production planners have good communications with sales to incorporate changes in the product and to schedule and plan production effectively?

Accounts and administration

Do you give credit too easily?

Would you lose in the end if you insisted on more cash payments up to a certain level?

Would the giving of cash settlements be financially viable?

Can you reduce credit terms?

Can you readily find out which accounts are overdue?

Have you got a smoothly operating reminder routine for outstanding accounts?

Are you oversensitive about insisting on payments, or about using a debt collection agency?

Is it necessary to keep customers who are always very slow in paying?

Are your prices and discounts related to the credit you give and the loss on interest that results?

Is there an overlong time lag between purchases and their accounts being sent out—are your 30 day customers really getting 45 days?

Are there any petty routines which can be axed—chasing tiny debts without regard to cost (as various parts of the Civil Service do), meticulous filing of endless trivial documents, elaborate internal communications?

Purchasing, Stock, Warehouse and Distribution

Is it worth keeping all that old stock—have you obtained maximum paper concessions for its depreciation?

Have you got a tried and tested system of communication between ordering, manufacture and sales departments?

Is your purchasing policy carefully thought out—are your bulk discounts really worth it when you consider cost of storage and risk of over buying?

Are you letting long habits prevent you from purchasing on more favourable terms?

Are your warehousing and distribution needs planned in unison?

Would rented warehouse space in many areas pay by reduced distribution costs?

Does your distribution coverage fall in with your marketing plans – does it make sense when considered in the light of your knowledge of market conditions?

Would rented or leased vehicles release enough capital for other ventures, to make this a worthwhile system?

Have you considered outside services for more remote or irregular distribution?

Personnel

Do the company's employees match the future plans for the company, or are they too high powered?

Do you have too many people in the company?

Would fewer, higher paid personnel be more productive than the present complement in all departments?

Have you worked out the costs and benefits of different salary structures, bonuses and productivity incentives?

Chapter 11 Raising the Selling Price

In your search for a higher gross margin, you might reach the stage of having cut every cost you can think of, and still not be where you'd like to be. Increasing the selling price will have the right effect and certainly seems a lot easier. It's a pity, of course, about competitors. Usually, if you up your selling price your competitors' faces are wreathed in smiles.

There are no easy routes to better business. Cutting costs is a difficult exercise—it's a problem to find places where they can be cut in a way that is effective while also not harming sales, and it almost seems inevitable that someone comes out of a cost reduction campaign less happy than he was before. If those are the burdens of cost cutting, then raising the selling price is surrounded by equal problems. The greatest of these is the uncertainty over the effect such action will have on the sales volume.

KNOWING THE MARKET

A thorough knowledge of the market is all important, for there is little that is easily predictable about any market. Buyers' motivation is of course a very important factor to consider. A luxury product costing about £20 is not likely to be affected by a price rise of 10 or even 20 per cent, nor will such rises affect cheaper, non-essential products—unless there is an equally well established competitive product available at a lower price. Even then, there is often that consolation of people assuming that a more expensive product, especially in the non-essential field, must necessarily be better than its cheaper rival. You might also be saved, in this category, by your competitors putting up their prices in line with yours, for there is often a 'follow the leader' element in price changes, whether by coincidence or collusion. The tempting thought of some other company enjoying the rewards of an increased gross margin (even though the facts themselves might reveal a less enviable situation) is one that easily prompts imitation, and then you will at least not have to worry about losing customers through price competitiveness. So competitors', as well as customers', reactions have to be forecast, guessed, predicted—or awaited at any rate.

When products are regarded as essential, the story is different. And 'essential' means different things to different people —an automatic washing machine is as essential to a stockbroker-belt housewife as a can opener is to a poorer housewife. Where there is a strong demand, there are competitors aplenty, and putting up your prices is likely to knock a large slice off your sales.

With everyone else in the field doubtless shouting about their fantastic bargains, is there any point at all in making your product more expensive? Well, perhaps yes. What you are concerned about is gross margin and overall turnover. Perhaps a price increase will hit your sales volume, but leave unchanged—improved, even—your annual turnover. With the same revenue from fewer sales you are in a much healthier position—lower expenditure, a lower break-even point. Trouble is, there is too high an element of luck in this. No matter how fine your judgement, how exhaustive your market research, you won't really know until you try it. Test market if you can, hope that others might follow suit, trust to luck that brand loyalty and snob value will compensate for the thrift of others. You could win—or lose.

JUSTIFYING AN INCREASE

All this uncertainty understandably puts off most people from a unilateral straightforward price increase. Ideally some disguise is called for. On one level this would be the sort that 'shoppers' friends' in the newspapers delight in exposing —different packaging, a slight increase in contents, an eventually discouraging special offer system—through which a marginal price increase remains undiscovered (aided and abetted by the comparatively generous margins of increase inevitable under decimal currency, if the product in question is a low priced one).

More honestly—and in the long term doubtless more effectively—something more concrete than illusionary should accompany a price rise. Of course, new packaging in larger quantities while keeping the same price proportion (20p for 1 lb, 30p for 1½ lb) is not a true price rise, but will give you the same effect, since your unit cost will have been reduced. Some change or addition to the normal product will also 'justify' the rise—some innovation to maintain a favourable value-for-money impression.

If a mild form of product innovation or better service is not possible, there are other possible ways out. You could compensate for lost customers by running a new advertising campaign, perhaps in a journal or paper whose readers you haven't yet tried to persuade. Be sure, however, that any additional advertising costs are built into the new price. Or perhaps an advertising campaign could announce your entry into a new market area where you would perhaps find things easier as a brand new supplier than one who has just increased his price. Again, the cost of launching in a new area would have to be taken into account, and most likely this cost would be high, the new area doubtless being some way from your existing territories.

More opportunities for price increases, and an overall increase of gross margin, could be available with a large product mix. A mixture of price cuts and price increases, perhaps establishing one or two loss leaders, could give the desired end result.

But usually increasing prices is a rather chancy way of looking for an increase in the gross margin. Even when your competitors, or one or two of them, are increasing their prices, it probably means that costs in general are going up and your increased gross margin would be temporary. Costs are going up so much and so often anyway, that you'll have enough trouble with those compulsory price rises without adding to them unnecessarily. If you do decide on raising your selling prices to increase your gross margin, do be ready with contingency plans should your grand plan misfire.

Chapter 12 Selling More

'Obviously'. 'It's all very well to say that'. Yes, this is the logical step and obviously it's what everyone in business spends half his time trying to do, directly or indirectly. Telling the chief of a company that the way out of difficulties is to sell more is akin to telling an ailing person that he will be fine if he gets better. 'That's all very well, but how?' Well, perhaps you haven't tried *everything* yet. Years of familiarity give experience and knowledge, but they can also fade away objectivity, and sometimes things get overlooked.

INCREASING THE STRENGTH OF THE SALES FORCE

Taking on another salesman is probably the quickest and easiest way of seeing whether sales can be sufficiently increased. You know how much revenue a salesman must bring in to make him a worthwhile 'investment' and results can be easily measured. It is even easier, of course, if you do not have products or services that require a long learning and preparatory stage before a salesman can do his job properly. And the investment can be reduced further still by a probationary period which is paid almost entirely on a commission basis.

A salesman can open and test a new market or a new product far faster than an advertising campaign, can be regulated and adapted in midstream, and can be stopped altogether, and abruptly, if things do not go according to plan.

Increasing sales force strength, however, does not necessarily mean simply getting more salesmen. It can mean increasing its effectiveness, by concentrating salesmen on more promising areas, moving them from both the 'easy' areas and the forever impossible areas. It can mean improved training, reviewing their means of remuneration to obviate any discontent and to ensure effort is rewarded.

NEW SELLING TECHNIQUES FOR NEW MARKET AREAS

Perhaps there are whole new ways of selling that you have not yet tried. Agents could handle your products in territories you would never get round to covering yourself. The returns might not be high, but it would all be something extra. Areas that do well through an agent could then be looked at with a view to direct handling and so bringing in a greater proportion of the revenue, but it is quite likely that a good agent will serve your needs for years to come. And for many, this is the only way to get into the exporting business.

If expansion into new and distant areas has too many complications, yet your product or service is locally highly successful, you might consider selling franchises, and so bringing in more revenue that way, even though you don't aim to be on a par with Wimpy Bars or car dealerships.

It could also be that you would get better sales results from a completely different approach—perhaps substituting telephone selling for direct personal selling. Lower costs and a greater number of calls could compensate for the higher percentage of no-sale calls to give a much improved overall result. Or perhaps direct mail advertising with salesmen following up coupon returns, or from coupons in newspaper and journal ads, would suit your business best.

With the emphasis on a quick improvement in the company's circumstances, some re-organisation of selling methods, and particularly of the salesmen is likely to be the most suitable path to follow. Appointing suitable agents and distributors could sometimes show rapid results with initial orders making quite a difference to your overall situation.

Other efforts to get sales moving quicker will take longer to give their full benefits, but could show some early results.

There are many different ways and means of advertising, and since they all rely on human response to an appeal of some sort, they will all forever continue to have a high degree of unpredictability. For this book, though, it is useful to highlight two basic types of advertisements—those which take up a few lines in classified sections or in local papers, and the TV ads, the newspaper, magazine and outdoor poster ads. The difference is not simply between the costs of the advertisements, enormous though that may be.

The first—the classified type—is really a 'for sale' notice placed where prospective buyers are going to be actively looking. It is unlikely that anyone who is not a prospective buyer will see the ad, and it is unlikely that anyone who does not see it, whether he is a prospective buyer or not, will know about the transaction being offered. If the items offered are subsequently bought from the source advertised, the ad has been effective. Even if the transaction is available elsewhere, it is simple to code the ad's reply address to measure response. It is always easy to see whether classified ads, reply coupon ads, the little ads in 'shopping by post' pages and so on achieve their purpose. Sales either result from them, or they don't. And the sales (or no sales) happen very soon after the ad's appearance. If results are achieved, the ad can continue, or reappear again when necessary. But if nothing happens, advertising can stop immediately.

With few exceptions, the other types of advertisements—the newspaper, magazine, TV, poster ads—are not so much 'for sale' notices as they are notices of information about products that are available. Ninety per cent of these products are available all over the place, and are being seen frequently. It is more difficult to decide whether sales are a result of the ads themselves, or of a number of other factors. Of course, it is easy enough to see whether the ad has had some effect or none—especially if no other major sales drive is on simultaneously. But how much effect, and was it worth it? That is much more difficult, and since these ads are so costly, tremendous care has to go into their wording, appearance, media selection—which makes them yet more expensive. So to get maximum effect (and to play safe) a firm doesn't just advertise—it has a campaign. Ads are preceded and followed by vigorous sales drives. Extra publicity is sought, perhaps packs are redesigned special offers are included, gimmicks thought up. At the end of the day—or month or half year—sales have gone up. Hopefully enough to pay for all the sales activity. But what achieved it? The pack, the salesmen, the free plastic daffodils, the magazine ads or the TV ad? For a couple of thousand more, you could probably find out—but the answer is likely to be a bit of each, and rightly so.

This is perhaps a long way to say 'Different needs call for different types of ads'. For the firm that is struggling to get back on its feet and even get one of its feet on the ladder again, the second type of ad, the glossy, glamorous one, is rarely the one to choose. There's no time to brief agencies, consider proposals, ponder schedules, plan publicity, think up gimmicks or offers. Nor is there money available. Half of all advertising at least is wasted, and any big advertising campaign is a risk—and this book is not so very concerned with taking on more risks. Besides, apart from the planning stage, the whole thing takes too long. Even if the campaign works, it might be too late. And if it doesn't work, you won't know until it's too late anyway.

But advertising can still play an important part in recovery—if it is used as a salesman. Study classified advertisement columns in newspapers and specialist and general magazines. Look at the 'shopping by post' pages in national daily and weekend papers. Look through the local papers in your market area, and in other areas as well. Then consider your products or services and see which ones could be advertised in a similar way.

Costs are low, but probably you will have to expand, or even set up, your own mailing department to despatch orders. However, by adding on postage and packing some of this cost will be recovered, and the savings of discounts and transport, etc., from your normal distribution will more than pay for the cost of this department, and leave some over to offer a 'bargain' price.

The ads themselves in mail order selling are worth studying, for they usually break all the 'rules' of the 'advertising establishment'. They are simple yet effective, waste no space, and universally mention at least one special feature, the price and some form of saving from buying by mail —either in convenience or, more usually, in money. Above all, their effectiveness can be very rapidly judged. (If you place ads in more than one source, don't forget some form of coding to trace replies. A common way is to include the initials of the paper in the reply address. Thus the ad in *The Sunday Times* will have your address as 'Nuts and Bolts (ST) Limited' and in *Exchange and Mart* it will be 'Nuts and Bolts (EM) Limited'. The cost effectiveness for your product of the different media will soon be discovered.)

Yet another type of advertising, even more selective, which can be considered, is direct mail. If you sell direct to industry it is quite likely that you are doing some direct mail already. There are many pitfalls in direct mail advertising. The most impressive leaflet or brochure, with the best possible copy on it, is no use unless it is actually seen by the right person. So you have to be sure you have the names of the right people —your mailing list has to be constantly checked and updated. Mailing to 'The Director', 'The Chief Engineer', 'The Buyer' doesn't do much good. Your leaflets and letters are your salesmen, and you'd never let them go into a sales talk without knowing the name of the person they were speaking to. Even worse, perhaps, is to use the name of the person who had the position two people and eight years back. Even taking these elementary steps is no guarantee of success. Direct mail has increased so much lately, and most people who have authority to purchase are saddled with so much reading, that most circulars, leaflets and other unsolicited mail goes straight into the waste paper basket—a weeding out process often done by a secretary, so that even a psychedelic envelope sometimes has little chance of catching the right eye.

If you think direct mail advertising could be right for you, bear in mind the main criterion for mail order and classified advertising—a lot of relevant information in a little space.

Your leaflet is your salesman—if you don't hook the reader in the first few lines, you'll lose him. So don't clutter up the envelope with four or five different sheets. And work out your costings on an expected three per cent response—anything over that and you're doing well.

Direct mail to the general public differs in some ways from direct mailing to executives at work. Name selection is just as important. Response rates from potential buyers is bad enough without wasting mailings, yet it's common enough for firms to send out leaflets for things like garden furniture to random names out of the telephone directory, half of whom probably live in high rise flats or urban terraced houses. The main difference is that you are not so hard pressed for time in which to get your message across. In fact there is sometimes merit in going to the other extreme. Once they've knocked off work, people have a fascination for brochures and catalogues (you only have to watch the exit at an exhibition hall to see how strong this fascination is), and a few glossy sheets with coloured pictures often finds a ready audience in the evening.

Without a substantial nucleus of addresses existing already, direct mail advertising is not likely to hold many attractions for the company that wants to get going again quickly, though there are service companies who will provide you with lists, or do mailings to selected categories for you, and can even help with the design of the leaflet and with the copy on it.

Of course it is impossible to generalise about advertising—the product, the type of customer, price ranges —everything has some bearing on the ads' style and its means of presentation. Posters, handouts, mail order direct mail, cinema, TV, all suit different requirements. The main considerations for the firm which needs to get established again quickly are time and money. Ads must work (or be seen not to work) quickly, and they must not require much outlay—at least until they are seen to be effective.

Publicity can also play an important part for the company in the stages we are discussing. The first reversal of past bad trends is something to be proud of, and worth shouting about. So let your local paper know, and send a letter to your trade journal. Short and to the point, and factual. Rags to riches stories are appreciated widely, but perhaps more widely appreciated are stories of people and firms who have come up again when all seemed lost. A lot of help can come, in rebuilding a company, from suppliers as well as customers. The more people who have confidence in you, the better, and a favourable write up in the press can work wonders.

Other publicity helps too—speak at local meetings, at Chamber of Commerce meetings, at conferences. Look out for imminent local events where perhaps sponsorship could get your name mentioned. It will help remove any stigma left over from bad days. Exhibiting at international trade fairs can be expensive, and usually has to be planned for well in advance, but local ones offer more opportunities, and even the big ones need not be ruled out if a stand can be taken in partnership with two or three complementary companies.

Chapter 13 Increasing Capabilities and Coverage

We've seen earlier on how too great a reliance on one product, or on one segment of the market can put a company in difficulties. Having all the eggs in one basket seems simple and convenient, but if the bottom falls out, there go all the eggs. So some diversification is a sensible precaution at any time.

HORIZONTAL AND VERTICAL DIVERSIFICATION

Diversification can also be a way up for the company that wants to rebuild and get into a position of strength and stability. There are two main types of diversification, known as vertical and horizontal (sometimes referred to as vertical and horizontal integration). The two terms refer to the direction in the cycle of production that a firm moves when it diversifies. Every product or service is at a particular stage of interrelated events. Horizontal diversification means staying in the same position in the cycle but widening coverage at that stage, while vertical diversification means moving along, or back, in the cycle.

The differences can be illustrated by taking a basic example of the cycle for garden furniture (g.f.):

Vertical diversification	*Horizontal diversification*
Prospecting for iron ore	General mineral prospecting
Iron ore mining	Copper, chrome ore mining
Refining iron	Manufacture of steel and alloys
Casting iron g.f. frames	Diverse foundry work
Finishing iron g.f.	Finishing wood, plastic g.f.
Selling iron g.f. to retailers	Selling household & g.f. to retailers
Selling iron g.f. to consumers	Selling garden equipment to consumers
Scrap iron dealing	General scrap metal, waste paper

Deciding on which way to diversify requires a close and honest study of your abilities and assets. A company selling garden furniture, and having an experienced sales team, good distribution facilities and enviable retail sites would be foolish to decide on vertical integration and go into garden furniture manufacturing. A well equipped foundry would stand a better chance of success if it undertook a wider range of foundry work, perhaps even going into glass-fibre mouldings, than if it decided to set up a finishing off department with its own retail outlets.

There are no hard and fast rules. It is as easy to find examples of sellers who have decided to manufacture one or more of the products they have been selling as it is to find manufacturers or wholesale dealers who have gone into direct selling. So upward vertical integration is not necessarily better or worse than downward integration.

Generally speaking, though, horizontal diversification is likely to hold fewer complications, and offer more immediate prospects than any form of vertical integration. After all, it is possible to spread activities sideways quite extensively without the fundamental skills being any different, and it can also be done more gradually, in smaller (less expensive) steps than any vertical movement. A service station that starts to sell confectionery and tobacco to motorists is doing a little bit of horizontal diversification that costs little and needs few new skills. To start a car hire department, though, is a very different matter.

COMPETITION

It's not only your own abilities that have to be taken into account when you are considering increasing your capabilities and coverage. Competition has to be looked at—possibly you will rule out horizontal diversification because all activities in this category are well taken care of, and instead see some good opportunities in vertical integration. The new markets must also be carefully looked into, for your knowledge and 'feel' of your own well known market won't be matched by what you know about the new areas. Another reason to take small steps at first.

BUYING EXPERTISE

But any new activity needs new knowledge. The easiest way to get both the new activity and the new knowledge at the same time is to acquire a complete organisation in that new field—a nice tidy package deal with premises and administration as well as experts and an established buying and selling system. Then you can take your time on refinements and rationalisation of administration, selling, etc. This might sound a big step for a company only recently in danger of going under or of being taken over itself. But the merits are often enough to outweigh the dangers. 'Horizontal' buying will give you far more resources, outlets, etc., which, if not entirely complementary, could doubtless be adapted, giving two similarly mixed concerns. Taking the garden furniture example again, a retailer of such products might buy a shop selling plants, seeds, fertilizers, garden tools and so on. It's an easy step to add furniture to the acquisition, and all the bits and pieces to the father company. Since this two-outlet empire is likely to give you an advantage over your competitors, backing for the purchase may not be that difficult to find, provided you are buying a sensible, going concern.

A 'vertical' purchase can be just as easy, since in your normal business activities you will get to know the organisations above and below you in the cycle, and are bound to pick up some of the expertise. (It would be a poor timber merchant who knew nothing of forestry, or of furniture manufacture.) You would consequently be fairly well qualified to judge the potential and worth of the purchase you are considering.

More likely than a straight purchase at this stage of your climb back to full recovery, however, would be a merger of some sort, and this is dealt with later, in Chapter 16.

In a previous chapter, going into new geographical areas was considered for boosting sales—this is naturally a way of increasing your coverage, and access to new areas could greatly influence decisions about diversification and about buying other companies to assist expansion. The owner of a hardware shop in West London is not taking many eggs out of his basket if he buys another hardware shop, this time in South West London. Certainly it is hardly diversification for though he is widening his coverage of potential buyers, he is still relying on buyers of hardware. Perhaps he would do better to make his second shop mainly home decorating, with hardware, keeping his first as hardware, with home decorating?

DEVELOPING NEW PRODUCTS

Of course, diversification such as we have been mentioning in this chapter might not suit everyone, especially manufacturers, and even those who want to diversify are not always in a position to do so in quite so radical a way. Or there might be no opportunities open for 'ready made' diversification. The development of new products might then be the only solution. Product innovation (and renovation) is, or should be, a regular consideration for manufacturers of every kind from motor cars to marzipan sweets. Such practices can, in different industries, form a major part of business activity, and lead times (the time from conception to sale) can vary from months to years, and require considerable planning and attention. We've covered this in our first book, and greater coverage will be found in numerous other books. But the company in a hurry should not rule out a new product to help it find its feet.

Of all the different ways of conceiving new products, from intensive market research to brainstorming and creative inspiration, perhaps the best suited for the company in the circumstances dealt with in this book is a mild form of plagiarism. The acknowledged masters of technical plagiarism are—or at any rate, were—the Japanese. They were in a hurry. There are hundreds of products made and sold all over the world that are not easily, or at all, available locally, and are not manufactured universally. Comprehensive reading of trade papers, local as well as from abroad, will unearth new products galore—ones that have gone through all the elaborate, time consuming and costly routines of trial and testing. Not all are patented world wide, not all have patents so embracing as to make adaptation impossible. And of those that are totally protected, some can easily be made under licence.

After much thought and deliberation, reading and talking, an enthusiastic company will come up with half a dozen feasible different ways of increasing its coverage and capabilities. How to choose which one to follow, if there is not one which seems to stand out above the rest? And even if there is one which seems to be just right, how do you justify it to sceptics? much depends on hunch, and much on luck—even the well and truly correct decision of 1973 can turn out to have been the completely wrong one when you reflect in 1976 after three years of unforeseen circumstances.

EVALUATING ALTERNATIVES

Obviously no-one goes by hunch alone, but even long discussions with plenty of 'on the one hand' and even more of 'on the other hand' can confuse the position instead of clarifying it. Best to be systematic about it, and even try and evaluate hunches. A good way is to draw up a list of all the factors you can think of which will affect the product, and those which the product will affect as well. Then grade each from minus for 'bad news' to plus for 'good news' giving points for five gradings. Like this, say, taking competition as one of the factors to be considered:

Competition

Market dominated by two or more major companies	−2
Market evenly split between two major companies	−1
One major company in market	0

Market evenly split between two or three ineffectual
    companies   +1
Market split between a lot of ineffectual companies   +2

These points numerate the various levels of suitability for
coming in with a new product, or going into a new area, or
diversifying into a new activity.

Similarly, you might have to consider production problems
affected by each choice. Grading could go like this:

Production
Needs completely new, unfamiliar technology   −2
Some new, unfamiliar technology   −1
New technology, but expertise available in company   0
No new technology   +1
No new technology and resources and capacity already
    available   +2

Do this for everything involved in each consideration—
distribution (all new outlets to no new outlets), sales (all
new salesmen to already having suitable sales force), company
image, brand image, buying resources, administration,
seasonality, market size, market type, buyer characteristics
and so on. Highest score wins.

Ideally this should be used for like compared with like
—different new products compared, different firms to consider
buying, etc., but much can be applicable for different courses
of action.

Whatever needs to be done, and whatever you want to do to
get the firm going again, is bound to require additional capital
or resources of some degree. The following chapters look at
ways and means of getting new money and resources.

Chapter 14 Utilising Existing Assets and Resources

Any substantial plans you make for putting your firm back on a firm foundation for future growth, after a particularly lean period, is likely to require outside finance. Existing resources will in all probability be few, or else well stretched. However, before any approaches are made to sources of finance, it is essential to make sure your house is in good order. So this chapter is useful as a preliminary to the next chapters, and as a means of reviewing that you have got your company running on smooth financial lines. You can expect that any outside source of finance is going to take a *long* close look at your company—if you can show that your resources are being utilised to their maximum, you stand that much better a chance of getting the help you need.

And, of course, you also have to face the possibility that you might not be able to get any backers just when you want them. The general economic conditions might restrict loans and overdrafts, others might lack confidence in your particular market, or they might want to wait longer to see if you can prove your firm's capabilities more convincingly. Or perhaps you might not agree to the terms conditioning any financing from outside. Getting the money might mean sharing control with the backers, or even losing it altogether, or perhaps tying you to policies you do not agree with. In these cases, you'll need to scrape together every bit of capital you can, and make doubly sure it is all being used to the utmost.

The measure of asset utilisation is its profitability. Every asset must make the maximum contribution to profits, and if this contribution could be greater if the asset was put to a different use, then, as long as it does not have an adverse effect somewhere else along the line, it should be put to that new use. A full study of asset utilisation calls for techniques more sophisticated than can be gone into here—work study, time and motion studies, value analysis, linear programming and so on—can all be brought into use, though it is always wise to consider the cost of some of the most time-consuming investigations. A value analysis done on a value analysis exercise itself could easily reveal that the cost will be more than the possible savings. But there are elementary steps which every manager should be able to take himself as part of his normally busy schedule.

In looking at resources and assets, it's worth splitting them into liquid and fixed assets, though it is perhaps more suitable to refer here to working capital instead of liquid assets, as some 'non-fixed' assets are much more liquid than others.

UTILISING WORKING CAPITAL

Stock or *inventory* is usually the least liquid of assets that come under the category of working capital. It might perhaps not be 'liquid' at all, and at best it will take a little while to realise. So it has to be watched very carefully.

There are a number of considerations to be remembered when you put your inventory position under scrutiny. The production department will be anxious to have a good supply of components or raw materials at hand so that production will never be disrupted through lack of supplies. The sales department will want a comfortable stock position so that it will never be caught with no stocks due to a sudden large order, or through the occasional inevitable production delays. Knowing how big to make these buffer stocks is a tricky business—further complicated by seasonal fluctuations, manufacturers' holidays, irregular delivery dates, lack of firm long-range commitments from buyers, possible short shelf-life of components, raw materials and finished stock, and, in some industries in particular, by short product life cycles.

The longer records have been kept, the easier it is to work out correct buffer stock levels. The rate of sale is known, the rate of production is known, and rough rules can be applied to availability and regularity of raw materials delivery. Put all that and more in a computer and you'll probably come up with an answer pretty close to what you can work out in your head. The important thing is to look at the factors involved and make a reasoned decision. Too often the buffer stock is an arbitrary figure which either puts the firm at considerable risk if there are any fluctuations from the norm, or costs the firm too much with too high a buffer stock. And it's not only quantities and run out times that have to be considered. If, say, raw materials are easily available, it does not always make sense to opt for frequent small deliveries. The cost of ordering say 1000 items from one manufacturer is no different from ordering 100 items—yet it is far more expensive to order those 100 ten times than it is to order 1000 once. If this ordering cost exceeds the storage and possible depreciation and risk cost of opting for the larger quantity, it is best to order the 1000.

Apart from it representing labour and materials paid for but as yet unsold, stock is expensive in its own right. A rule of thumb to work by—if you haven't done more exact calculations yourself—is that stock costs about 12 per cent of its value. Thus for every £1000 worth of stock, the firm is losing £120. This can often offset bulk buying discounts—a bigger stock means more staff in the warehouse, more storage equipment, above all, more space.

Once you have satisfied yourself about stock levels, routine precautions are essential. Buffer stocks must be kept at the agreed level. If you have agreed on quantities, then stocks must be adjusted to compensate for affecting circumstances, and the only way this can be done is to keep a perpetual inventory by recording movement, and double check this with regular stock takings (throwing in a surprise one now and then to discourage malpractice). Stock depreciation can be reduced by always following a first-in first-out policy. With some stock this can be combined with a buffer stock check by having a two bin system. As one 'bin' is depleted with outgoings, the second is filled. When the first is empty, the second is used, while the first is topped up. At any one moment, you should always have one full 'bin' (or shelf, cupboard, rack, room).

Labour forms a major asset—in many cases the bill for wages and salaries is the biggest item of expenditure every year—yet it is often treated as something completely different. Yet it is vital that maximum utilisation is obtained from this large cost. This is not to advocate slavery, but the realisation that a happy and contented work force is always more productive than a disgruntled one. A high turnover of staff loses a company vast sums of money. Recruitment and selection is expensive, training is lost money if the new person leaves after a year or so. No sensible manager would buy machinery for thousands of pounds and then neglect it. Computers are tended anxiously in air-conditioned rooms, plant is maintained and polished. People need looking after too. And that also means recognising their strongest features, and using them. A 'born salesman' forced to be a marketing manager, is a wasted asset. A first-class production man put into a purely administrative role is a wasted asset. Beware the Peter Principle!

But there is the coldly economic side that is more easily identified as well, and perhaps never more easily in industries susceptible to frequent work load fluctuations. Builders have this sort of problem—one moment they have plenty of work for 150 people, the next moment their buildings are completed and there's a two month wait for the next major job. If all 150 are on the payroll, it either means laying them off then going to to the expense of recruiting again, or keeping them all on, but idle. Both expensive steps. For the small business, that sort of operation no longer holds any future, and the only possibility is to subcontract, and become a co-ordinator.

Cash in hand, and at the bank, is naturally the most 'liquid' of all assets, yet there is no particular merit in having thousands of pounds in your bank or in the safe. Cash is fine and comforting, but unless it is working for you, and earning its maximum profit, simple possession is a wasted opportunity. Just as in private life many people boast that they've 'never owed anyone a penny', so many companies religiously keep a very favourable bank balance and more than cover current liabilities with liquid assets. They would regard a current liquid assets to current liabilities ratio of 1:1 as treading an uncomfortably narrow path, and aim for a ratio of at least 1.5:1 Those playing safe in the extreme would not put too much faith in counting debtors as fully current assets—a cynical but realistic attitude, for some debtors are no more 'liquid' than stocks. So they would aim to supplement debtors substantially with other current assets to have a very safe margin over current liabilities, the major part of which would be amounts due to creditors.

On the face of it, of course, a current assets to current liabilities liquidity ratio of less than 1:1 means that a company does not have enough liquid assets to meet its obligations. But this would often be the ratio in those many other companies who believe in always operating with a substantial bank overdraft. There is a lot to be said for getting your bank in as deep as you can. Getting the maximum overdraft is easiest when times are good all round and your position looks most favourable. Even though that's also probably the time when you least need a big overdraft, it's worth getting it—if you don't want to invest it in any expansion just then, it can always be put to some use, and you'll have it available when you need it later.

But more about this in the next chapter—the point now is that you have to decide whether you are going to work with a liquidity ratio of 1.5:1 or over, or work with an overdraft and have a liquidity ratio of less than 1:1 (the ratio gets doubly harmed for not only do you not have actual spare cash in hand, but the overdraft appears as a liability—short term at that—on the balance sheets). Having decided on your policy, stick to it and get the maximum use from it. Simply deriving mental satisfaction from cash in the bank doesn't justify such a step if you could be getting some returns by employing most or all of that cash. Similarly, if you decide to work with an overdraft, you have to satisfy yourself (and any potential backers) that your return on that overdraft money is higher than the interest you are being charged.

Debtors can constitute a large part of the assets in a company's books, so they too must be properly managed. Having large sums of money owed to you means a lot of money that is really yours that can't be used. Giving three months credit means letting someone else invest your money for their own gain for three months—so don't be more generous than is absolutely necessary in giving credit. By reducing debtors accounts as much as possible, you are getting maximum use out of your returns from production. Apart from this 'free lending', you are running the risk of 'free giving' if you do not run proper checks on your customers' credit-worthiness. The rules are—ensure credit-worthiness fix the smallest possible maximum credit terms, stick to agreed settlement dates and insist on them right from the start—and make the whole business run as quickly as possible by prompt sending of invoices and statements. If you are giving 30 days to pay, but only get round to sending out invoices a month after purchase, you are really giving those customers 60 days' credit.

It you want to be rid of the debtors problem altogether, you might even be able to hand over the whole lot to a factor at an agreed exchange rate, as we point out in Chapter 15.

Creditors are on the books as liabilities, for you owe them money to which they have a real and early claim. But they are —or can be—very useful resources and so should be properly utilised. Really this means doing a reversal of what you do about debtors. Now it's your turn to get the best possible terms from the people who supply you with your needs. But getting maximum use out of creditors doesn't always mean simply getting the longest possible time in which to pay their bills. If you are given 3 months to pay a bill of £100, with the alternative of paying cash of £90, it is only wise to take the 3 months if you are sure you can get that £100 to earn more than £10 over the 3 months (a bit more than more, strictly, since you could be putting the £10 saved in the cash discount to some work as well). Besides, most purchases in any company are fairly regular, and from fairly constant suppliers. Getting credit is only advantageous once. With £100 purchases each month, once the first 2 or 3 months is up, you will still be paying £100 a month, every month. In many cases you will find that your supplier will be so pleased to get a quick payment that you should be able to negotiate some other condition which is more advantageous to you—cash discounts, packaging concessions, deliveries, preferential treatment during shortages, etc.

UTILISING FIXED ASSETS

Property and premises are just about always the biggest of the fixed assets, and again you must be sure you are getting maximum profitability from them. For this, it is essential to know the true current value of the property, even though balance sheets do not have to show current values, but normally show the original purchase value. But it's a false security you feel if you boast a 20 per cent profit on the value of the business when in fact the value of the property might have increased considerably—your profitability could easily really be 12 or 13 per cent. If the overall value of the business has increased proportionately far more than profits over the years, the company's profitability has really declined.

A good way to redress the balance could be to put this major fixed asset to a different use. One way could be to sell the property, to an investment company perhaps, and then to lease it back at prefixed rents. There will be the advantage of having the rent allowable for tax, and a sizeable amount of cash which you could use for financing expansion. But once again you have to ask yourself whether you will be able to put this cash to good use—a use that will bring in a better return than the increase in property value. In most cases, property is such a sound investment that selling and leasing back would only be done if cash was urgently needed for carefully planned purposes, and it couldn't be got hold of elsewhere.

But there are other steps which could be considered to make sure this fixed asset is being used profitably. The surroundings might have changed considerably since your business started—are you still in the most suitable area? Have rates increased substantially? Has your distribution been altered by local changes, or changes in your main market's location? Are you still close to the right source of labour supply? Perhaps selling part of your property, and moving part of your business elsewhere would give advantages. Or move altogether, as so many have done from the London and South East area. With the sale of a central property added to development area grants, less expensive wages and salaries bills, you could have a far more profitable business.

Plant, machinery and *equipment* can form as big a proportion of a company's fixed assets as property. Are you getting maximum life and use out of them? Unlike property, plant very rarely appreciates in value—it is only general inflation that perhaps slows down the real depreciation of some plant. But that need not be borne in mind when depreciation is being charged on the balance sheet, so you must make sure you are charging the right amount for depreciation. Much specialist plant calls for caution. Some activities have very unfavourable resale qualities. A foundry, for instance, might be on a site which is appreciating attractively, but the premises will be depreciating pretty rapidly too, and there's not much anyone can do with an old foundry—except use it as an old foundry. Special-purpose machinery will also have a low, or non-existent resale value, and any new activity calling for such equipment should be considered with this in mind.

Expansion carries many problems with it as far as plant and equipment is concerned, especially in smaller companies. A small printing works with two printing machines that decides to buy a third machine is increasing its capacity by 50 per cent. It is going to be quite a while before it can step up its orders by 50 per cent as well, which means its equipment will be running well under capacity. Such under-utilisation is inevitable—small firms just have to go up in leaps—but it must be anticipated and taken into account when planning expansion. There are two paths that can be followed to escape the worst of such under-utilisation. You could delay the purchase and subcontract work until you are getting in enough orders to use up most of the idle time, or you could arrange to do sub-contracted work yourself at only marginally profitable rates. (And it is not only the machine that would be idle, but its operator as well—both expensive items.)

Vehicles can also be a large item in the list of fixed assets. At least their current value is able to be determined more easily than that for plant or premises, which often require expensive valuations to get an accurate figure, and they are more 'reliable' than most plant and equipment is. All the same, is the money tied up in vehicles being put to the best use? Many companies are turning to fleet purchase schemes, which on the face of it may seem more expensive. But there are advantages in having agreed repurchase prices at a predetermined time, known maintenance costs, and less expensive administration from doing away with constant buying and selling in small numbers. Straightforward hire of vehicles is also administratively less expensive and releases capital for other uses. And hire is an ideal system, especially for the small company, when expansion means that you need, say, another one third of a vehicle. Hire can give that one third vehicle, whereas buying another vehicle would result in a two thirds under-utilisation.

Consideration of vehicle utilisation should also cover much of the field covered when reviewing premises. Resiting a warehouse might only give small advantages as far as property assets are concerned, but it might make a world of difference to the number and type of vehicles required. It might take you nearer to a suitable rail head, for instance, or cut down on expensive through-town routes.

It's always easy to find some way of getting capital from your fixed assets, and in these sophisticated 'service economy' days there is often a way to have the same sort of facilities as before you sold our own. But there is no point in getting loads of money unless it is going to be used more effectively than it was used before, when it was tied up in fixed assets. The main thing it to be sure that all assets are being utilised to the maximum. Besides, fixed assets are security to outside sources of finance, who will look both at the assets themselves and at their utilisation.

Chapter 15 Getting Financial Help

Raising capital to help a company get back on its feet after it has been down but not quite out can be more difficult than raising capital for a brand new venture. There is some excitement over a new company, and the hopes and determined intentions of its founders can encourage backers. Too often, though, backers will hesitate when it comes to investing in a company that has already been in the doldrums. What can happen once. . . .

But there also can be sympathy for people who make a comeback, provided they display the same qualities of confidence and determination that characterise successful entrepreneurs. In any selling game, confidence is vital, and in trying to raise finance you are selling yourself and your company.

Product knowledge is also a requisite in selling, so you have to have all the facts about your company at your fingertips —and be ready to disclose them. Woolly words like 'considerable' and 'substantial' are overworked, and too often cause sceptical reactions. No investor worth having is going to put in money without knowing exactly where it is going and what it is going to be used for. Not only will he want to know about the company's present position and your intentions, but he will want to know about its past as well.

So take along sales figures, profit and loss accounts, and balance sheets for the past five years for interested parties to examine. This will allow them to verify your reasons for your company's bad times, and they might also be able to point out a few other things you weren't aware of. Either way you stand to gain.

A third important factor in selling is product features, so in selling yourself and confidence in your company's future you must have something of note to offer. It's no use asking for backing to let you carry on along the same old path that has already led you into a few marshes, and there's not much hope if you sound like just another little company trying to keep out of the red.

If possible you should have something that distinguishes you from your competitors—a new product, a new piece of equipment that will allow you to cut costs, or manufacturing times. But most of all you should have something that distinguishes you from your company as it used to be—a carefully prepared cost reduction programme, a plan for re-siting which will halve distribution costs, a new method of work organisation which will step up production, a new pricing policy, a more efficient accounting and debtors control set up, a much more efficient warehouse.

PREPARING A BUSINESS PLAN

What all this means is that you must prepare for your fund raising just as carefully as you would if you were out to get a vital new contract. The best way to do this is to prepare a 'business plan' which you can show to the people you are going to approach. For this business plan, you should list summaries about:

The history of the company.
When it started.
Who has been involved in its direction.
Summary of its growth (you'd be taking recent balance sheets with you as well).
Development of the market and competition.
Major changes and developments.
Reasons for stages of notable growth or decline.

The present state of the company

Who the key people are—their jobs in the company, their qualifications and experience, length of service, conditions of contract.

Current position in the market, and who the market leader is; state of the market.

List of assets and liabilities, sales analyses, costs breakdown or management ratios, especially gross margin, breakeven points etc.

Details about special equipment and machinery, and, if machinery plays an important part, assessment of condition and future usefulness.

Production facilities, which machines under full load etc.

Research and development in progress.

Main suppliers and main customers.

Number of existing customers, potential customers etc.

Any contracts you are negotiating for, or which you expect to bid for.

Plans for the future

Detailed exposition of what capital is needed, and exactly how it is going to be used.

Details of your 'formula for success'—the key feature which is going to make the future better than the past.

Projected budgets, and cash flows, and profit and loss forecasts.

Critical factors which can influence future developments for good or bad.

Market research findings for future growth.

Contingency plans in event of changing circumstances or competitive action.

Future staffing and labour needs.

References—key people who have advised you, or who are in other ways anxious to see your business grow.

SOURCES OF CAPITAL

In our book *Enjoying a profitable business* we mention the main sources of capital—banks merchant banks, etc.—and these are usually well known anyway. If you've been in business for some time you will be on familiar terms with your bank manager already, so doubtless will go to him first—and a few other banks as well, if yours can't help. Then you can do the rounds of merchant banks (if you are in that league), ICFC, investment grants, and so on.

It's when you've drawn a blank at all the traditional sources that you have to start thinking hard about other ways to get the money you need, and this is where a well prepared business plan can pay dividends. You can use it to try the offbeat areas, remembering that every pound helps.

Directors of bigger companies in your field, or in companies that supply you, are sometimes quite willing to put up some money in the hope of getting a good return—but consult your solicitor about the wording of any letters you send, for you can't write letters which invite people to subscribe for shares.

The big tycoons of business and industry are all household names, and probably get hundreds of letters from people in all walks of life from charities to cranks, but that is no reason why you shouldn't try them as well. All of them have got to where they are by having a nose for a good business venture, and your plans might appeal to them. They are also involved in dozens of companies and might be able to suggest another source, or perhaps assistance in the form of supplying against later payment.

Retired directors often still like 'to keep their hand in' and might find your company interesting. If they've been in a similar type of business to yours, you could also get the bonus of their experience and advice.

Solicitors and accountants advise their clients and frequently administer trust funds, and invest capital on their behalf. Your appeal could catch their attention.

Your suppliers and subcontractors have an interest in the future success of your company, and might be able to invest a small amount.

And try all your friends too—every bit helps.

SUBSTITUTES FOR READY CASH

Getting money in the form of ready cash gives you a pleasant feeling of independence, and seems a tidy way to begin the 'new era'. You might not be able to raise as much as you would like, however, and so you'll have to think of other ways of getting the equivalent of ready money.

We've already seen how hiring vehicles can release capital, but these days you can hire everything from carpets and chairs to Caterpillar tractors. If much of your capital needs is ear-marked for purchases of equipment of any sort, leasing could get you what you want without capital, and usually you can get just as much choice as you can as if the capital was your own and not the leasing company's. Of course, you don't own the equipment, but payments are tax-deductible.

If your suppliers can't help you with a straightforward loan, you might be able to persuade them to give you very extended credit, at a favourable interest rate, for goods you get from them. If your regular suppliers can't help at all, why not look around at some others—the number two's (if you've been dealing with number one), the new ones in your area. With the promise of your future loyalty, and if they think your company has got a future, they might stretch a point in your favour.

Liquidity problems often seem as if they would be solved if only one company, somewhere, would pay his bills. The eternal complaint is 'I'd love to pay my bills, but I'm waiting for someone to pay me theirs. As soon as I'm paid, I'll be able to settle my debts and have money for re-investment'. Unfortunately overdue debts and bad debts are here to stay, so long as credit is given. But factoring can ease the burden. Factors 'buy' your debtors' invoices from you for a percentage of their amount and then it's up to them to get the money. You have the advantage of being paid cash for all your sales, even the credit ones, though of course you don't get the same amount as for an ordinary cash sale. Still, if it means getting rid of all those debtors problems and cutting down on the administration work, it could be an attractive price to pay, as well as being a way to raise ready money.

FINDING 'TIED' MONEY

If at all possible, you will want to keep control of your company, but the overriding need might be for capital, and you might be forced into parting with some of your autonomy, and taking a partner. A number of institutions which provide venture capital insist on one of their nominees joining the board of any company they invest in. Private individuals might also want to have a say in the running of your company as a condition of their investing in it, or want to appoint someone to keep a watching brief for them. It's unlikely that you'd object to this, since it is a reasonable request (if the investment is substantial), and you'd be getting some brain power added to your board at no extra cost.

This also raises the partnership question. If you don't have luck getting money with few strings attached, you might get what you need by offering a partnership. There are quite a few people with money who would like the independence and authority of running their own companies but haven't got quite enough capital to set up entirely on their own, or are too old to start a company from scratch, or are specialists in an already fairly crowded field. A partnership could be the ideal answer to their aspirations, and also solve your problems.

Of course, there's a lot more at stake in getting a partner than in simply taking on an additional board member: you'd have to make sure you could get on well together, and would see more or less eye to eye on important issues. But two heads are frequently better than one, and through your partner's contacts and possible other interests you might be able to expand your activities and your markets. Look for them in the same way you look for private investors—trade directories, Institute membership lists; Company House records and so on.

SOMETHING FOR NOTHING—OR ONLY A LITTLE

While you're considering types of financial help other than ready money, you should also think of all possible 'money alternatives'—ways of getting what you need without using too much capital. Try not to buy anything if you can hire it, borrow it, be given it. Universities and technical colleges can often help with research of many kinds: you might not need or be able to afford a research team—or person—for year after year, but you could get contract jobs done by a College or University, or you could take on students for vacation jobs.

Professional institutes are often a source of help with papers and reports, and can recommend people who might be able to assist you with particular problems. The trade press can be a cheap way of learning new techniques and discovering hints, and most offer an advice or contact column. Big companies can frequently pass on information which you will find useful, and there are numerous Government and other official or semi-official bodies which have advisory activities.

The main thing is to cast your net as wide as you can, and gather it in frequently. There are few problems which have not cropped up before, so someone, somewhere, is bound to have a solution. And money isn't always everything—even if it seems to be the only thing that is going to help you. When you have worked out carefully exactly what you need the money for, let your imagination roam freely—both to see where you might be able to raise the money, and to see if there are ways of reducing the amount you need.

Chapter 16 Merging

If you baulked at the idea of a partnership, you are unlikely to take kindly to suggestions that you merge with another company, for you are likely to lose even more autonomy. But beggars can't be choosers, and besides, you might be able to arrange a merger which will really make little difference to your responsibilities and freedom of action. A proper merger should open new fields, new possibilities, new challenges and new opportunities. But the danger is that it might resemble the definition of the verb—'lose character or identity in another'.

Selecting who to merge with is therefore extremely important, and of course you should be certain that some form of merger is going to be the best way to get your company back on the rails. Naturally there has to be some loss of identity—a merger is, or should be, a mutual business, and the other firm will also be reluctant to lose its identity. Give and take on both sides is called for.

CHOOSING A MERGER PARTNER

Drawing up a short list of merger prospects is like short listing new products or services, and considering diversification. You have to decide how far you want to diversify, and whether you are going to go vertically or horizontally. The degree of diversification in a merger is likely to be fairly limited—broadening your interests into very different fields is likely to be better achieved through taking a share in different companies.

So you have to consider, first of all, your *competitors* in your area. If you combine, are you likely to have a higher combined turnover than the present sum of both firms' sales? Will such a merger put you in a position to tackle a market leader, or will it be a merger that's aimed at forcing down competition? If the merger makes the new company the market dominator, it might lose a lot of sympathy—and orders—and leave itself open to whittling-away action by small competitors. It's always tempting to merge to create a near monopoly situation, but it's a move that seldom seems to pay off in the long run. Not if you also want to enjoy your business, anyway. Far better to get together to have more strength to tackle the 'big boys'.

Merging with an old enemy has its advantages, of course. You lose a competitor and gain an ally. You probably already have a good knowledge of the company, its people, its customers and its methods. But it has disadvantages too. Your salesmen will be faced with the problem of extolling the virtues of a product they were recently comparing unfavourably. You won't be doing anything really new, and sales increases, once they are divided, are unlikely to be much different.

The savings, of course, come from rationalisation. Salesmen, administration, production, warehousing, and so on can be reduced proportionately. But that brings endless human problems—sackings and redundancies, and the businessman who shrugs these off in the name of progress and profits is becoming rarer, even if he is a wealthier person. Besides, it leaves a lot of people in the area who are definitely not going to be customers of the new company.

The other thing about merging with a competitor in your area (if you are using a merger as a way to get back after being in the doldrums), is that you are more than likely to get the worst of the deal. Your competitor will know your circumstances, and will have the upper hand. You will be trying to sell yourself, your company and its prospects. But it will be a buyers' market, and the buyer will know it. You'll find yourself making concessions and will quite likely land up not so much with a merger, but with a mild takeover—with the other firm doing the taking.

Far better then to look for a similar company in a different area, or one in your area but in a different segment of the market. Use the merger as a means to expansion rather than a means to salvation—but get your salvation through expansion. If you go for a company like your own, in a different area, you will be doing a straight forward market expansion, but would still be able to rationalise on some outgoings, even if it's only to the extent of getting better deals through purchases in greater bulk than before. With less dependence on one market area alone, and with proportionately lower expenses, you could carry out some price cutting, or be able to afford more intensive advertising and promotion, and so eventually increase your sales in your own area. You'd also be more likely to keep most of your original independence—provided, of course, that the other company didn't think your past hard times were due to your own incurable mismanagement.

There's also a lot to be said for a 'diversification' merger —not into a different area, but into a different activity. Follow any thread suggested in Chapter 14. You could merge with a wholesaler if you're a retailer, or vice versa. If you are in the consumer field, you could merge with someone selling similar products in the industrial sector. You could merge with a manufacturer if you are a distributor—or vice versa. Whatever level you are in, you could merge with someone at the same level in a slightly different activity—such as a ladies' dress shop merging with a men's outfitters; a toy shop chain merging with a sports shop group; an electrical component manufacturer merging with a manufacturer of electrical guages, and so on.

PROBLEMS OF MERGERS

The vital thing to remember about a merger is that the new company must have greater prospects than the sum of the two companies' individual prospects. Otherwise there's no point in merging.

Selecting a short list of firms you would like to merge with is, however, the easiest part of this route to recovery. If you don't want your company to lose identity, and also want to stay on with it, you will have to go about your merger hunt in the same way as you would look for capital to be invested in your company (see Chapter 15). After all, you have got to put across a convincing argument about the future of your company, and clearly show that past ills are over, and that a merger is exactly what is needed to get the pendulum swinging the other way. Not only that, but you have to show why and how a merger is going to help the other company. Quite a hard job—not unnaturally, a growing company with a history of steady advancement makes a much better merger prospect than one which seems to be looking for a merger to keep it from decline.

A merger approach, to have a chance of success, needs plenty of preparation; a business plan such as outlined in the previous chapter, a detailed analysis of future prospects for the new organisation. You won't have time to prepare a future plan to go with five or six approaches, but informal approaches to the heads of the companies on your short list will at least sort out who is prepared to go into detailed discussions.

And never forget that you are selling—so emphasise the benefits the other company will get from the merger. And base your approach on all the facts you can get—from Company House records, from friends and business associates, from your salesmen.

But perhaps you won't be able to tempt anyone into a merger, or perhaps their terms put you off. Failing everything else, you'll have to think about selling your company.

Chapter 17   Selling Out

Getting rid of the company altogether doesn't sound much like a route to recovery, but recovery means that future days will be better than the immediate past ones, and this can come about from selling the company. It certainly holds a lot more hope for everything and everyone comprising a company than simply closing down does, so it is worth considering.

Whether the top people, the major shareholders, in the company stay on after it is sold, is up to them. Even if they leave, personal recovery is still possible—in new fields. Although no-one likes selling something that is close to them, and which represents years of labour, owners of a company also have a duty to their employees, and should try to keep the company going, even if it means selling their holding, if the only other alternative is a steady decline.

PLANNING TO SELL

So if you find yourself in this position, it's worth putting as much into the sale of the company as you would into any plan for its future success, and, like any sale, it has to be planned. The causes of the company's decline, and therefore the reasons for selling, will affect your approach. A declining market is likely to mean that you can't look to your competitors as being prospective buyers—in fact they might be about to come on the market themselves. If you have to sell in a hurry you won't have time to carry out much pre-sale planning, but if you have seen inevitable decline coming, and don't want to try to salvage the company yourself, you can dress things up a bit by cutting back on non-essential expenses and so getting a more reasonable profit figure.

But elaborate deception is pointless—'second hand car' practices don't often work when companies are being sold. The main thing is to pick prospective buyers carefully, using the same guidelines as you would when looking for a company to merge with, to draw up a short list. The big difference, though, is that you won't have to limit your choice to firms of a similar size, as you would when considering a merger. While another small company may just be able to offer takeover terms that suit you, your eventual purchaser is likely to be a medium or large company.

When you are looking for a likely buyer, don't skim over the small companies in similar fields—ones that look like suitable prospects, except for their size—until you establish who actually owns them. Many small companies are owned by large holding companies, and if this is the case with one of those that seem suitable, the holding company is a good bet as a buyer. Here you would also stand your best chance of keeping things more or less the way they used to be. Of course you'd have a lot of head office participation, and would doubtless have to fall in line with new administration and accounting procedures, but the outcome could be almost as attractive as if you had found a source of capital—provided the holding company had faith in your management team.

CHOOSING YOUR COMPANY'S FEATURES

While you will ideally be trying to sell the company as a going (relatively) concern, you should also be realistic about the sale. We've said there's no room for deception (the word gets around quickly), there is everything to be said for strongly emphasising the good points. A realistic assessment of these might indicate that insisting on the 'going concern' approach is not going to do too much good. A whole hotch-potch is usually less attractive than some smaller amount of quality. A small diamond is worth more than a wheelbarrow of broken bottles. Your 'diamond' might be your customers and your goodwill, it might be your premises or your machinery. It might simply be your patents or licences. The thing is you must decide on the 'product features', and angle your selection and approach to match.

Selling out can mean a lot of lost pride, and if you stay with the company it'll mean forgetting a lot of the past and throwing everything into the new set up—perhaps learning to operate quite differently, and accepting someone else's ideas. Or it means starting again from scratch. If you start all over again, or decide that a complete sell out is still not the answer, and none of these eight routes is going to apply to you, you could set your sights along the ninth route, and take a gamble with luck.

Chapter 18   Contingencies and Last Resorts

'Forecasting' said a Chairman recently in his annual report, 'is very hazardous—particularly in relation to the future'. There can't be a businessman anywhere who doesn't wholeheartedly agree with that statement. Research, forecast, plan as much as you like, you still never *know* what will happen tomorrow—let alone next year or in five years' time.

You could plan any, or nearly all, of these past eight routes to recovery, but at the last moment all the plans could be made worthless. Markets suddenly slump, new discoveries can make your methods, materials, techniques or philosophies obsolete. Sources of finance can dry up so suddenly you think they must have been mirages. The company you were going to merge with gets taken over by a firm that doesn't want to know you, or the company you were (as seemingly a last resort) going to sell to suddenly finds it has been getting its sums all wrong, and puts itself in the hands of the Receiver.

If all your plans go wrong, or equally depressingly, none of these routes are going to be possible and you can't even sell your company, what can you do? Well, it helps a lot if you are prepared—yes, plans again, contingency plans. Very pessimistic businessmen will perhaps also have further contingency plans in case the first contingency plans also come unstuck, but very pessimistic businessmen aren't often very successful. Optimism is a prerequisite of achievement.

PLANS AND PRODUCTS IN RESERVE

But even the supreme optimist must have one plan in reserve —which means if your primary plan goes wrong and you operate your contingency plan, you should, as soon as possible, work out another plan to fall back on if something new happens. It's a wise precaution—too many wrong decisions can be made if the pressure is really on hard, and usually you will be too preoccupied with the emergency of a changing situation to spare the calm deliberation necessary for planning ahead.

The precautions of contingency plans should, if possible, be extended to the practice of having your 'recovery' eggs in more than one basket. For a company that is getting back on its feet, that is not always possible. Resources are bound to be limited, and the strain put on them by any one plan might forbid any distribution in another direction. You may well have to put everything you've got into, say, developing a new product, and simultaneously carrying out a strict cost reduction programme or a massive selling effort on existing products could endanger the success of your new development.

Generally, though, there is bound to be some mixing of the various routes. Getting financial help will be that much easier if you can show a maximum utilisation of your fixed assets, have instituted strict cost reduction measures and have careful plans for the development of new products or services. Then if you can't raise capital, even if you have to delay your new products, you could perhaps keep going until conditions improve enough to get the loan you need, or until you can look into the possibilities of a merger, or being bought by a holding company.

But it is still possible to be in the position where everything depends on the success of one solitary plan. In the case in the above paragraph the major plan could have been the success of the new product—raising the capital being necessary to get that plan into action. What can be done if the product fails? Or what if, even after making the company as efficient as possible, you still cannot raise money, merge or even sell the company? What can you do when all the plans come to nothing?

Well, this is a book about rescuing and reviving companies, so there's going to be nothing about how to wind up a company, how to go into liquidation, how to go about being declared bankrupt. Surrender isn't a last resort—it's what happens when the last resort fails, and this book will presume that the last resort doesn't fail.

A shipwreck makes a fitting analogy. Survivors follow the lead of whoever shows the most initiative, gather together what can be salvaged that will be of use, and make for the nearest bit of land affording shelter. There they assess their situation, establish a relatively stable community, and see how they can get themselves back to civilisation.

When a company begins to founder there is often time to do some saving and salvaging. Many of the employees are bound to be lost, but you could try to keep a group that will be of the greatest future use—a skeleton staff representing the different talents that will be needed. Ages would not matter—younger people might be happier to accept the challenge and compensate the risk of a survival struggle with the potential of seniority if the struggle pays off: older people could bring years of experience (and perhaps the experience of earlier working with less sophisticated methods and machinery) and accept the risk against the uncertainty of finding a new job.

A new strategy will have to be worked out. Depending on the reasons for the downfall, it could be to start up in a new field, a different branch of the previous activity, or the same business as before. A new start is an ideal chance to do something entirely different, and there is no better way of choosing the first choice than by deciding what you would most *like* to do. Start with ideals and wishes—short listing is the time for wondering whether or not there would be much chance in that activity. Have brain storming sessions with the skeleton team, with everyone putting forward suggestions as fast as possible. Don't worry about can and can't, possible and impossible, sensible or foolhardy. Not yet.

Then list all your liquid and fixed assets and your liabilities and see what the most is you would have over. See what could be salvaged. Perhaps the sale of your premises and half your equipment would clear up all your liabilities. Companies have been started on less than two lathes and a delivery van. But make sure you know exactly what will be over, in realistic terms. A special piece of equipment might still be worth something substantial in terms of the old company, but for the future it might be worthless and perhaps unsellable.

Your list of assets remaining should then have added to it the most important assets of all—the abilities and experience of the skeleton staff. Don't leave a thing out for seeming to be irrelevant. The fact that your sales manager made his own glass-fibre hull for his sailing dinghy could help. If you and your team are really determined and dedicated, other assets could be listed now—how little each of them will require at the start, in return for shares in the company. The gamble they are taking is a considerable asset, and a low wages bill will also be an asset.

Your search for assets should be as wide-ranging as your random ideas about future activities. Of course, much depends on how big your skeleton staff is, how many assets you have left after a projected sale of the company: but there are assets hidden all over—private cars, large outbuildings at a director's home, a couple of portable typewriters, wives who can type, do accountancy work, sell, manage outworkers. Imagination is a very valuable asset.

Investment grants are other 'assets' to take into consideration—if you can operate from the relevant areas, the grants can give you the boost you need.

Then, when all your assets and potential assets are listed, you can short list your potential activities and look further into them. If you are keen on an investment area, you'll have to investigate local markets or assess transport costs. Competition will have to be looked at, costings done, viability worked out. And don't forget past satisfied customers and suppliers. Even if you decide to set up some new activity, they might still be potential clients and give you an early break.

And when you've settled on your new plan, there is no reason why you shouldn't look once again for venture capital. Your plans to revive your old company might not have attracted sources of capital, but your new scheme might. You could be at the start of an exciting new business—the silver lining to the cloud of the old company's decline.

Chapter 19 Looking Ahead

There's no getting away from the fact that every year hundreds of companies go bust, but hopefully the previous chapters have helped you to rescue your company in time. With immediate danger past and indications that there will, after all, be a future, it is never too soon to look and plan ahead.

In our previous book, *Enjoying a profitable business*, we go in some detail into short-and long-term planning, and generally try to supply, as the subtitle implies, *a practical guide to successful growth techniques for small companies*, and we hope you will find useful information to help your company's future growth. But your present greatest need is to consolidate your position, to establish a firm base on which to expand your company, and make it more profitable—and enjoyable.

Earlier chapters in this book went into causes and symptoms of failure, and gave hints for the prevention of their occurrence (or recurrence). Your first downward trend may have been due to factors entirely beyond your control, but there is no reason to suppose that 'lightning does not strike twice', so you should always be on the lookout for all symptoms of decline. And if the decline was due to some internal mismanagement, it is equally wrong to expect you'll spot it and deal with it sooner. Bad habits do have a way of recurring. But nor should you be so wary to symptoms and causes that your business begins to stagnate.

All so easy to say. But a good motorist keeps a sharp

lookout for all hazards, and not only the one that last scared him—and a good motorist does not crawl along at 20 mph when conditions favour a higher speed.

CONTROL DOCUMENTATION

If there is one thing that helps to highlight all the different symptoms of decline, it is an adequate control documentation system. The period of consolidation is an excellent time to draw up such a system. Without it you won't be able to monitor your achievements, measure your results, properly plan each step—or see symptoms of decline. Decide on a cross section of management ratios which will measure your sales and expenses, stock turnover, production costs, profitability, etc., and stick to them, also working them out for past years (if you haven't already done so to discover the reasons for past decline). Whenever you work out a special plan or undertaking, simultaneously draw up a method of measuring their progress and comparing it with the desired level. Departmental budgets must have their controls, their comparisons of expenditure and income, and must be measured in relation to other departments' performances.

But never go overboard on control documentation—the important thing is to select the key figures to keep an eye on, and have them presented in such a way that an easy comparison with past figures is possible. Usually it is comparisons and trends that matter, rather than figures themselves. Some managers give personal assistants or trainees the job of keeping charts showing expected against actual performance, or present against past. Ten key charts brought up to date weekly, fortnightly or monthly, can be looked at in half as many minutes, and extra time need only be spent on looking into variances.

LONG-RANGE PLANS

Mainly, though, you will want to use your period of consolidation on planning ahead—first of all a long-range plan, and then a detailed plan for the year ahead.

To some degree, your long-range plan will already be

mapped out, as the steps you took to get the company back on its feet will have considerable influence on the future. You might have started a new product range, or moved into a new area—your long-range plan will then perhaps be mainly to establish and expand the product or area, but you will have to estimate how long the expansion could carry on, and what you will do when it has reached its peak.

If your recovery has been achieved by trimming costs and doing some concentrated selling on your existing products, then you will be aware that this is a 'forced' situation, without very good long-term prospects. Your long-range plan is therefore bound to cover the development and launching of new products or services, or the expansion into a new market area.

Long-range plans must cover the results you want to achieve and the results you expect to achieve—that is, you must have a clear idea of where you want to be in five years' time. It's only half a plan to decide to try to achieve a growth rate of 5 or 10 per cent a year, unless you are satisfied that that is exactly what you want. You can't always do what you want to, but you should try. Things which make you disgruntled now are likely to still make you disgruntled in five years' time—more so. Long-range plans should map their disappearance and the introduction of things which will make you more contented and interested. Growth is important—but enjoyment is as well. And growth is easier if there is more enjoyment.

Having decided on where you are going to try to get to, plans must concentrate on how. The ways can be as diverse as the routes to recovery, and you could find that, having rescued a declining company, your long-range plan is to sell the company and move into a different field, or perhaps to alter the whole character and activity of the company.

For most, though, future intentions will doubtless be simply to have 'more of the same'. But how will this be achieved? Questions need answering:

How is the competition likely to develop?
What changes in the market are likely?
How will these changes be met?
How much of the product and market life cycles is there left to run?

What new developments can be brought in to meet growth targets?

What is the likely lead time for developing and introducing new products and services?

Are there likely to be any major changes in the availability of materials and supplies?

What new equipment and plant is going to be needed, and when?

How will this be paid for?

How much extra staff will be needed to handle expansion?

Will new specialists be needed—what is the availability of personnel?

Can the increase of output be gradual, or will expenses and maximum outputs have to go up in steps?

Could turnover match these jumps, or will each expansion period have to be saved-up for, or will subcontracting absorb temporary excesses?

What are the long-term requirements for premises—will the present locality be able to meet these requirements?

Are there any restrictions (other than the size of the market) limiting the potential of your company?

Would it pay to move elsewhere to escape these restrictions, or is there any way at all of getting around them?

Long-range planning means knowing where you want to go and how you intend getting there. It embraces all activities in a company and tries to anticipate the needs and performances of each—personnel, production, premises, sales, services, supplies. It means never being caught out by anything except the truly unforeseeable, for long-range planning also means drawing up contingency plans—so that you aren't caught out when predictions or gambles don't go off as expected. It means thinking ahead towards everything from raising capital or going public to changing the company image or moving into new export markets.

But obviously long-range planning is no magic solution to business problems. Planning something is no guarantee at all that it will happen—the opposite often seems to be the case, and some argue that the future is so unpredictable that it is not worth planning for. Certainly there is little point in spending hours and hours each month dwelling over hypotheses and

mathematical models, and drawing up targets for five years'
time. The value of long-range planning is in the thought that
goes into it. Having a clear mental picture of what you are
trying to achieve makes it that much easier to make detailed,
short term decisions, for then everything is seen in relation to
clear objectives.

Another motoring analogy can put long-range planning
into its proper perspective. A driver setting out to motor from
London to Scotland by way of the Midlands, doesn't worry
about how he will get through Birmingham until he gets there
and concludes his business in that city. His immediate objective is to get out of London—which he won't do very successfully if he doesn't bear in mind that he wants to get to
Birmingham. But, knowing that he has a long journey ahead,
he will have prepared for it by having his car serviced, and by
getting road maps which cover the whole trip right to Scotland. Each stage of the journey will bring him closer to his
objective, but he won't get out his road plan for the centre of
Glasgow until he has actually got there. And, of course, somewhere on the way he might have a breakdown, and have to
change his plans, reaching his destination by train instead. Or
he might meet a wealthier acquaintance who will offer him a
lift in a chauffeur-driven Rolls Royce. The methods of getting
there might have to change, but without the long-range plan
of getting to Scotland, he'd be an aimless motorist wandering
around England.

SHORT-TERM PLANS

If the intent to get to Scotland is the motorist's long-range
plan, the routes he takes through the towns and the country-
side form his short-term plans.

While some may argue that all a long-range plan needs is
some vague idea of intentions, no-one can deny the importance of careful short-term planning, or budgetary control. To
start a year without objectives, targets, expenditure ceilings,
and a monthly plan of action is putting far too much in the
hands of luck—and luck rarely looks after anyone for 365 days
every year.

Budgeting and budgetary control is covered in considerable

detail in our other book, as is long-range planning, and there are many other books as well, some devoted entirely to this subject. There is far too much involved to deal with it in only a few pages; besides, everyone practises some form of budgetary control, and it needs to be studied in depth the better to refine it.

But it is worth emphasising here the importance of careful short-term planning. A company which has just got out of hard times and is consolidating itself is still in a precarious position. In the same way that doctors prescribe stringent post-operative conditions, and keep regular watch during recuperative periods, you will have to lay down strict conditions to ensure effective consolidation. New investment will doubtless soon be necessary to finance expansion or new products, and the profit objective will be an important item of the short-term plan. And for profits to come anywhere near their planned level, everything else has to fall into place—turnover and expenditure throughout the company has to be planned, and, above all, monitored and controlled.

The short-term plans are the essential formulae you apply to make your business work, and perform as you want it to; the control documentation you set up is your indicator of whether all is going according to plan, and the control panel that lights up when something goes wrong. No business can function long without either the plans or the controls.

In this book we've concentrated on recognising symptoms of decline in small companies, on identifying their causes, and on ways of reviving the business. Only briefly have we touched on the running and building up of a small company, though obviously the methods used to revive a company are similar to the methods used to keep the company in good health. Many other things which might help to keep a company profitable, and the running of it enjoyable, are covered in our first book, and it would be wasteful to go into them here. But there could be some further clues and aids to revival in the remainder of this book, which highlights some of the opportunities to prepare for in the new business life of the Common Market, and relates three case histories of successful revivals of flagging fortunes.

Chapter 20 New Opportunities in the Common Market

Few issues in recent years have produced as many words, articles, arguments, and opinions as has Britain's entry into the Common Market. The temptation to ignore it all and let someone else get on with it is great—there are enough other things to worry about.

But it's not difficult to look on the bright side—after all, if something is going to happen, the only thing to do is make the best of it. And making the best of it could mean, for many companies, the difference between stagnation and growth, decline and salvation.

One of the first things to do, though, is to get hold of a copy of the booklet produced by The Confederation of British Industry (21 Tothill Street, London SW1). *Small Firms and the Common Market* is short and simple, but worth reading in detail, and it will allow you to get rid of most of those articles you've been putting aside for reading 'when you get time'.

Small firms stand to do better out of the Common Market than most large companies do, because so many small companies are subcontractors to large companies. With the Common Market, there are going to be so many more large companies on your doorstep. If there have always been about 100 companies forming the possible market for your products, you could find that you will now have 500 potential customers.

And many of them will be no further away than some UK companies already are—and no further away from you than they are from small companies in the other Common Market countries. Remember, trade barriers will disappear. And with container facilities, roll-on roll-off shipping, and the East and South East ports, transportation costs and distances will be little different from, say, Birmingham to Brussels, than they will be from Dusseldorf to Brussels.

Many small companies, unable to get above about 60 per cent of full load, have often looked wistfully at the export market. Often, though, difficulties from trade barriers, documentation, payment, etc., have outweighed the attraction. With the Common Market, most of the problems will be removed, and it should be possible to step up that 60 to 80 per cent.

The same will go for companies supplying finished goods to distributors. Past years have seen steady rationalisation of distributing organisations into a few major ones. The Common Market will redress the balance, and 20 outlets could easily increase to 100.

Getting into those other 80 should be relatively simple for UK companies, whose products are frequently superior to those made on the Continent—and often less expensive as well, because of lower labour costs here. True enough, labour won't stay cheaper for long, but that is an added incentive to get in quickly on a competitive price basis, and hold the advantage with superior quality.

Small companies should also be able to avoid the stigma of strikes causing late deliveries, as this reputation usually rests with larger organisations. Anyway, strikes are as frequent in most of the Common Market countries.

Not that it's going to only be plain sailing, of course. It is often emphasised that going into the Common Market will give efficient companies opportunities to grow bigger, faster, than they could otherwise—and will make it harder for inefficient firms to stay in business.

After all, there are several thousand small companies in Europe looking forward to Britain's membership to give them a chance of getting at *her* manufacturing companies, distributing organisations, and consumers. Cross-Channel container ships won't come back with empty holds, distances are the same both ways, and tariffs which now protect local companies will go as fast as those which now make Continental customers seem remote.

So it's no use pretending there aren't difficulties which will have to be overcome. But, as in everything from wallpapering to mountaineering, preparation is of paramount importance. Customers must be looked for, but Britain's entry is a national entry, so there is no shortage of help available from Government departments as well as from many other official bodies.

Language barriers needn't be too much of a problem. It could be worth getting together with other similar companies in your area to get translations of selected articles from the trade press in other countries, and even to undertake joint selling trips. Services and joint enterprises should be used wherever possible, for there will be too much different at first for small companies to 'go it alone' altogether. Advertising will often need special thinking (apart from translation) and packaging could need extra attention. Reactions to everything from humour to design vary enough throughout Britain as it is —it is all too easy to make unintended howlers when different nationalities are involved.

Going into the Common Market countries will need all the same care and preparation that you would give if you were going into exporting. But so many of the difficulties of exporting will be absent that in time other countries will seem like other counties.

Efficient companies should have nothing to fear, and everything to look forward to.

Chapter 21   Three Stories of Recovery

COMPANY A—FINDING NEW CONCRETE PRODUCTS

Markets can suddenly 'disappear'—often through no fault of your own. This happened to Company A. Along with other precast concrete manufacturers, a large slice of its market disappeared after the collapse of concrete cladding in a tall block of flats in the London area.

For the larger companies, it was only a part of their market which had vanished, but smaller companies were very seriously affected. Many went out of business. Company A fell between the two extremes—it kept going, but lost the very substantial amount of £30,000. Something had to be done urgently, otherwise it could not carry on for long.

Specialised equipment gives a lead

The first step was to establish precisely the advantages the company had with its special plant and handling equipment. With concrete products, a key issue is weight and handling, and delivery costs are naturally a major item. Products are specialised and varied, and inevitably different companies develop different facilities. This company had equipment capable of handling 10 ton items, and could deal with dimensions as large as 8' × 6'. They decided to go for the large-sized end of the range.

Next the company had to consider the types of concrete

products falling in this range, and it was decided that flooring offered a reasonable potential in the present difficult market climate. Experiments were made with minimal thickness floors, and the company developed a floor with two layers separated by polyurethane foam. This system would allow concrete to be poured into the intervening space at the site, giving it the necessary strength. It would also be possible to leave ducts for cables and pipes within the floor.

Items for stock smooth workflow

Any activity to do with the construction industry is plagued by uneven work loads, and so the company also decided to have a range of products which could be manufactured for stock. These included concrete blocks, various kinds of paving slabs, and other concrete products for the garden and do-it-yourself market.

Estimating's key role

The company prepared a new leaflet describing its special facilities, and mailed every potential customer within a 30-mile radius. The object was to get as many enquiries as possible, and though the estimating department was frequently overloaded, it became possible to get one order out of every 10 submitted estimates, by adjusting prices according to work in the pipeline.

Adjusting prices gradually, the estimating department slowly but surely improved the ratio to one order for every five estimates submitted.

Estimating, incidentally, can be a critical part of a small company's activities. Many have to estimate for almost every order. Close examination of the reasons for failing to get a particular contract should offer a guide to the estimate for the next contract, and in nearly every case this should lead to an improvement in the ratio of estimates to orders received. Many small companies owe their success to the recognition of the importance of estimating, and it is frequently the personal responsibility of the principal to agree the final figure, relating it always to the capacity likely to be available at the time delivery would be required. In contracting work, there are many costs which can be varied, by necessity if not by choice.

Fruitful search for new products

A final step for Company A was to search for new products which could be made out of concrete, but which were currently being made out of some other material. Technical magazines, from overseas countries particularly, were examined for ideas. The company's salesmen were briefed on their approaches to architects and civil engineers to see if there was any construction product which could equally well be made out of concrete instead of its usual material.

These searches bore fruit when an architect put forward a suggestion for an interlocking concrete 'brick panel'. After the usual teething troubles, and some marketing problems, the first order—for 900 to be built on external bathrooms—was received.

From then on, the company has never looked back.

The main lesson that can be learnt from this simple case study is that much vaunted management techniques played hardly any part in the company's recovery. It was ideas that gave Company A new opportunities.

This is true of so many company success stories. Small companies rarely become successful because their managing directors are experts in all the latest sophisticated management techniques.

But this case also shows that there is no magic about new ideas. Some people obviously do get more ideas than others, just as some are inventors. But looking for new ideas connected with present activities needs no special gift.

COMPANY B—A CHANGE OF WIND FOR A DRAUGHTPROOFING COMPANY

The popularity of double glazing has resulted in many small firms specialising in this business in the early '70s. In the more austere '50s a similar objective saw many firms selling draughtproofing of doors and windows with phosphor bronze strips tacked to the frames.

Increasing installations of domestic central heating added to the sales arguments of draughtproofing, and a minor boom in this market developed. More and more firms sprang up and competition became intense, with sales reached by local press advertising and direct mail, followed by door to door salesmen —who even resorted to cold canvassing.

Competition and idle time close companies

Small companies soon began to get into difficulties through one of their biggest dreads—idle time. The product had to be installed promptly (because of strong competition) and this meant that some weeks were overloaded while in others there wasn't enough work for the installers. Many of these small companies went out of business.

Company B was one that was about to go into liquidation. The owner complained of his problems to a friend and was advised to think of another product—preferably a 'do-it-yourself' one—suitable for the same market, but able to be sold through retailers and wholesalers. He bought phosphor bronze strip in bulk, packaged it in cartons with 20-ft rolls and the necessary tacks and instructions. Fitting this system was a difficult job for the average householder, and the scheme was only moderately successful.

But it helped to keep the business out of the red, and it also showed that a large market was there—if only a simple product could be evolved, which any householder could fix, and which could also be an 'impulse buy' product.

A product variation is instant success

Many searches and thoughts later, he came across poly-urethane foam, which was just coming onto the market as a soft mounting material, for use in upholstery, etc. The possibilities struck him at once. He got hold of a manufacturer who could fix a self-adhesive backing, and had the product he'd been looking for. All he had to do was package it in a see-through plastic bag, with an attractive label and an easy to remember name, and he was back in business.

In a big way. With one type of pack for the hardware trade and another for Woolworths, quick eye appeal and a low price, it was an instant success. Which of course attracted competition. To keep ahead, he dreamt up many more uses apart from draughtproofing—stopping rugs slipping, fixing on the back of pictures to keep walls from getting marked, and so on. He also started a semi-industrial market. But the main market was obviously domestic, and a variation of the product, rather than the use of it, was needed. He thought of a threshold—a metal strip with a soft plastic covered polyurethane foam affixed.

Getting out while you're ahead

Once again Company B was successful. And once again competition caught up. Now the owner thought up a plastic flap to go along the bottom of a door, but this was not nearly so successful.

Ideas were running short, and though profits were still good, the writing was on the wall. His next bit of good sense was to sell the company.

At the time of writing the company and its original products are still in business, as part of a large organisation. But it hasn't grown, and it's doubtful whether its profits are anywhere near as high as they were 10 years ago.

As in the previous case, ideas played a big part in Company B's salvation. But the main point is that when there is an expanding market, selling a fast moving product with a high gross margin gives you the cash flow for rapid expansion —provided you are one of the first in the market.

As soon as competition develops, try to devise a second product that you can sell on the back of the old. If this is closely linked, you can enclose leaflets for the second product with packs of the original, and get 'free' promotion.

Finally, when you run out of ideas and the competition is baying at your heels, sell the company.

COMPANY C—BUILDING UP A BRICK COMPANY

Company C was also plagued by the ups and downs of the building industry. (Ups can be as bad as downs, for then there is inevitably a shortage of materials.)

But it was a slack period which did the damage. With demand falling off rapidly, the company carried on making bricks for stock, without looking into how this would be financed. And since slack periods are often accompanied by high bank rates, the cost of financing this stock became unusually expensive.

Problems in forecasting slumps lead to overstocking

Manufacturing for stock for too long is an easy trap for small companies to fall into. Reluctant to lose skilled labour or to have people doing nothing, they work on the basis that the market is bound to change for the better soon. The failing is to incorrectly forecast the duration of the slack period.

A rough and ready guide to booms and slumps is the four year cycle which is to some degree influenced by politics. Usually a change in Government when times are bad will push the economy up. And with a steady Government, things tend to get really bad before effective measures are taken. In either case the pendulum takes a long time to complete its swing.

So if you believe you are at the bottom of the curve, you should reckon on a lapse of four years before true boom conditions will prevail. The intervening period will, of course, be a gradual improvement. Similarly it would be a naive businessman who, after a boom period of a year, invested heavily in a project that depended on the boom being just as good in four or five years' time. Nothing lasts forever.

Company C not only got its sums wrong on the state of the market, but it also made another of the manufacturing-for-stock errors—it didn't take precautions to see that its stock didn't deteriorate. By then the bank was also putting on the pressure, and with a new management coming in, decisions had to be taken fast.

The first thing had to be a risk—cutting down the labour force and shutting certain kilns. To get the stock moving, a good sales force had to be built up quickly. The management went into the field, and even one or two people from the production side.

The next most urgent task, to start rebuilding, was to get a clear view of the market. The sales for the last six years were analysed, and salesmen reported types and sources of all their customers' brick supplies. Lists were prepared of potential customers.

Reviewing the market shows a break

The company had in the past sold both to builders and builders' merchants, and it now decided that the jobbing builder was the one least likely to be affected by the slump in new houses. Since the jobbing builders buy direct from builders' merchants, who are normally safe business risks, the company decided to concentrate on the merchants. The catchment area was increased to bring in as many builders' merchants as possible.

With stock moving at last, the next step was to alter the product mix, according to indications from their analyses, from 90 per cent commons and 10 per cent facings, to 70 per cent facings and 30 per cent commons. The difference in costs for making facings and commons was slight, but the facings have a higher selling price, so there was an improvement in the overall gross margin.

This couldn't be done overnight—experience had to be gained in the number of facings which could be made, as the mix of brick within the kiln had to be changed. Being old-fashioned, the works were very labour-intensive, but a change to pallet loading and the use of forklift trucks cut costs and speeded up operations.

In less than two years, and even before the market improved, the company went from loss to profit. In the third year the market recovered, and the company made record profits.

This case shows how careful you have to be about manufacturing for stock. It is seldom an answer to any problem, unless you change products for stock (and ones that don't deteriorate), for once conditions improve you still have to shift your stock as well as your current output. And this can't often be done.

But perhaps even more it illustrates the need to constantly review the market. If Company C had kept a close, constant check on its market, it could have swung its emphasis on to merchants well before it got into trouble. It could also have changed its product mix and improved its profits which could have helped it to ride out even a severe slump.

Even in boom times, markets and sales mixes should be

continually reviewed, so that you are sure you are getting the best available return. After all, it's much easier to strengthen your position when conditions are good and your bank manager is contented, than to re-organise while you are also skimping and saving.

These three cases are isolated ones, and perhaps very different from the sort of conditions you will be faced with. Yet they show how three companies in seemingly hopeless conditions were revived without massive injections of capital, in market conditions which were anything but favourable.

Perhaps yours will be case number four.

CAN WE HELP

By examining the past five years' balance sheets of a small company, it is possible for an experienced person to indicate ways and means whereby its profits could be improved. Your own Auditor may be able to help and guide you, but if you feel the authors could help, all you have to do is to send these balance sheets to Small Company Techniques Limited, Wivelrod Farmhouse, nr. Alton, Hampshire, allowing 14 days before you receive their recommendations.

A fee of £50.00 is payable only if you are satisfied that the advice given is a worthwhile investment.

Index

Index